FOOTBALL
IN
THE
1980s

FOOTBALL
IN THE 1980s
THE

MICHAEL KEANE

Cover illustration: Wimbledon's Vinnie Jones gets to grips with Newcastle United footballer Paul Gascoigne during their League Division One match, 1988. (Mirrorpix)

First published 2018

The History Press
The Mill, Brimscombe Port
Stroud, Gloucestershire, GL5 2QG
www.thehistorypress.co.uk

British Library Cataloguing in Publication Data.
A catalogue record for this book is available from the British Library.

ISBN 978 0 7509 8118 7

Typesetting and origination by The History Press
Printed and bound in Great Britain by TJ International Ltd

ACKNOWLEDGEMENTS

Thanks are due to several people who have helped me put this book together. Firstly, thanks are due to the staff at The History Press, Beth Amphlett, and Mark Benyon, for commissioning and publishing my book. Secondly, thanks are due to my brother Gerard, whose idea it was for me to specialise in the 1980s, and also to my other siblings, Bridget, Richard, Mary and Stephanie, for helping me navigate the decade in one piece. Finally, I would like to thank my own team at home, my wife Gabby and our children Thomas, Oliver, Patrick and Annabelle, who are the stars of my show.

Michael Keane

INTRODUCTION

This book was written almost by chance and certainly for fun. The chance is easy enough to explain, as I will try to, and hopefully the fun will come in the reading of it.

Some time last year, on some errand or other, I found myself trawling through assembled junk in my attic. Once up there, I started to browse around to see what detritus I had insisted on keeping for years. After rummaging through various boxes, I soon found myself staring at the cover of one of my favourite ever singles, 'My Perfect Cousin,' by The Undertones, (it reached no. 9 in March 1980, in case you need to know). Whether you know the track or not – though God himself is rumoured to have it on his personal jukebox – does not matter, as it was the cover not the song that sent me spinning back into some serious nostalgia. On that cover is the unmistakable, spindly figure of a Subbuteo player. He is wearing red and white and has a full house cheering him on. This chance discovery sent me racing to find first my old Subbuteo set – just two drooping goal nets and scores of broken players remained – and then, in the next shoebox along, my old programme collection. It was almost entirely from the 1980s, as I drew the line at paying more than £1.00 for a programme many years ago!

Flicking through various old programmes transported me back in time; in an instant, I was once again tuning into *World of Sport* with Dickie Davies; I was enjoying the wrestling on a Saturday afternoon with my dad; I was listening to the football scores on my tiny transistor; and I was playing with my personally customised Subbuteo set. I had managed to travel nearly three whole decades in the ten minutes me it took me to hop up my attic ladder.

I gazed at programmes featuring badly permed footballers; I cringed with dismay at the fact files documenting players' favourite meals and actresses; but I warmed to the memories of long-forgotten games that had seemed magical at the time. I had got the nostalgia bug and I couldn't shake it. In fact, I got it so badly that the idea for this book first germinated and then started to grow.

I hope readers will share my enthusiasm for a decade in which I personally gorged on football. I feasted on FA Cup Finals, wondered at World Cups and simply shook my head at the state of the stadiums. All told, though, it was great fun for me to revisit memory lane and I hope you enjoy the trip too ...

LOCK STOCK AND BOTH BARRELS

In the 1980s there were some things you just took for granted: Margaret Thatcher won general elections, Liverpool won the league every year (almost), and Wimbledon won all the prizes for roughing up their opponents. Tales were plentiful of the The Dons' antics under the stewardships of Dave Bassett and Bobby Gould: newly-arrived players found their suits were cut, on special occasions players were deposited in car boots and some poor souls were even tossed into canals!

Set against that background of pushing every boundary, the events of an afternoon at Plough Lane in February 1988 are not so hard to figure out. Midfield bulldozer Vinnie Jones was tasked with man-marking Newcastle United's new kid on the block, a blossoming genius called Paul Gascoigne; he was not so much a bog-standard midfielder – more of a footballing Gandalf, with the tricks, twists and touches of a footballing wizard. For Jones, the afternoon's assignment was a bit like being asked to try and catch the wind, but not quite so easy.

Faced with the impossible job of nullifying Gascoigne's brilliance, Jones hatched a plan of his own. Eschewing all recognised tactical nuances, the Dons destroyer instead focused on the basics, and decided that, when the referee was not looking, he would cut off Newcastle's supply lines by simply grabbing Gazza's testicles. As the game petered out into a fairly drab 0-0 draw, Newcastle's number eight was indeed unable to conjure up any great moments of magic, and so, not for the last time, Jones' utilitarian approach enjoyed a measure of success.

The moment was captured in an image that almost defines the time it was taken in. On one side we see a stony-faced, snarling Jones, seeking any advantage he can muster as he squeezes the life out of an opponent. Then we see the victim, a still cherubic Gazza, wincing and grimacing, as his talent is temporarily reduced to rubble. Way back in the 1980s, in the days before uber-fit athletes and superstar players dominated, football could still make room for all sorts – for artisans and artists, for Jones and Gascoigne, for the good, the bad and the ugly!

ALL SIT DOWN

In the 1960s, under the management of Jimmy Hill, Coventry City quite rightly earned a name for innovation. Sky Blue Specials took travelling supporters on the train to away fixtures, the Sky Blue Pools raised cash and if that wasn't enough you could also ring up Sky Blue Rose for the latest club news. Those innovations had Hill's trademark vision all over them and in 1981 he was at it again as he oversaw the planning, design and completion of England's first all-seater stadium, at Highfield Road.

Increasing disturbances, both nationally and locally, had persuaded the Coventry board that something had to be done to remedy football's biggest ill. A combination of all-seated spectators, all-ticket matches and increased prices (£1.50 tickets rose to £5.00 if bought on match days), was the strategy, as City planned to price out the troublemakers and appeal to a new 'family audience'. The opening day of the 1981/82 season saw real optimism as Dave Sexton's young team beat Manchester United in front of a capacity crowd of 19,329. Briefly it seemed that Hill and Coventry might just be on to something.

Sadly, within weeks Leeds United fans found alternative uses for the shiny new bucket seats, hurling them in all directions; it seemed troublemakers could still make trouble whether standing or seated. The early season optimism soon gave way to some bleak realities, as attendances dipped and disturbances continued sporadically. The first season with seats saw crowds drop almost 20 per cent, and a similar drop in attendances in the second year left the Sky Blues averaging a miserable 10,500 per home game. The well-intentioned and undeniably brave experiment was at best faltering and at worst failing.

Two years after Highfield Road had gone all-seater, Coventry's board accepted what seemed like the inevitable and decided to partially open the Spion Kop terrace; the scheme had obvious flaws – high pricing in a recession-gripped city was pretty obviously never going to work – but the fact the scheme was attempted gave just a glimpse of what a different type of future match-day experience could be like. Sadly, it would take later events at Hillsborough to force football to understand that change was needed. Coventry, like the rest of the footballing landscape, had just not been ready for the future.

THE GAME OF SHAME

The World Cup in 1982 is fondly remembered for many things – that dazzling Brazilian side, Paolo Rossi's unparalleled marksmanship, even the tumultuous semi-final between France and West Germany might all spring to mind. One other memory, however, is a less welcome reminder of an otherwise excellent tournament. A match was played in which the normal rules of trying to outscore your opposition were lamentably ignored when West Germany met Austria in their final group match.

West Germany's campaign had started dreadfully with a 2-1 defeat against unfancied Algeria, it was the first time an African side had beaten any European team, and it put the German's pre-match predictions of seven or eight goals into sharp focus. Germany did improve, easing past Chile 4-1 in their next outing, while Austria steadily progressed with two successive victories.

Because West Germany and Austria did not play until the following day, when Algeria won their final group match the two European teams had time to race to their calculators to see what result would suit them both. A narrow German win would secure both their own progress and Austria's, thereby eliminating Algeria. Though the scenario was clear, not many predicted what would pass for a football match the following day in the heat of Gijon.

When European Championship star Horst Hrubesch nodded Germany ahead after ten minutes, the game ended as a contest. The early 1–0 score line suited both teams, guaranteeing each a slot in the second round, so they simply stopped playing. For the remaining eighty minutes, over 40,000 fans whistled and jeered and waved white handkerchiefs as the teams endlessly passed sideways and backwards, mostly without even an opponent within 10 or 15 yards. The idea of a football match was simply abandoned as cynical pragmatism won the day.

Viewers of the match were united in their condemnation of both teams. French coach Hidalgo observed the teams could qualify for the Nobel Peace Prize, while unrepentant German boss Jupp Derwall argued that his only objective had been to progress to the next round. The game though did have one lasting legacy, however, as afterwards FIFA changed the rules to ensure all final group matches be played simultaneously, to avoid further outbreaks of collusion.

THE NUMBERS GAME

It has often been said that you can prove anything with statistics. While that may or may not be true, the following list of head-turning stats might give some food for thought ...

£1,469,000 was the British record transfer fee as the 1980s started. It was paid by Wolverhampton Wanderers to Aston Villa for striker Andy Gray. At the time Wolves were a moderately successful top-tier outfit, but the transfer showed their increasing ambitions. After signing on in September 1979, Gray went on to score the winner in that season's League Cup Final victory over Nottingham Forest and, for a time, the skies above Molineux looked as golden as the team's shirts. As the decade went on, though, the club's debts and playing fortunes both spiralled out of control, and after three successive relegations Wolves found themselves in Division Four by 1986.

Twenty-nine matches unbeaten from the start of the season was the run Liverpool's 1987/88 vintage enjoyed in a league season of unparalleled excellence. Kenny Dalglish's men equalled the then best-ever unbeaten start set by Leeds United in 1973/74. Bolstered by new signings Aldridge, Beardsley and Barnes, Liverpool were simply a class above most of their opponents as they produced fast-flowing football with a style and a swagger not always associated with previous, more efficient Anfield teams.

Ten straight wins was the blistering start to the league season that Ron Atkinson's Manchester United team made in the autumn of 1985, with five of the victories being by three goals or more. FA Cup holders United simply tore into their opponents as they hit an irresistible run of form. Goals were shared out between Robson, Stapleton, Whiteside and chiefly Mark

Hughes, but wherever you looked United seemed to have goal threats, and after an eighteen-year wait it seemed as if the league title was surely on its way to Old Trafford once again. Despite winning thirteen of their first fifteen matches, United's title charge hit the rocks when engine-room skipper Bryan Robson endured prolonged lay-offs. A collapse in form that extended well into the new year saw United's title hopes splutter and choke before they finally limped home in fourth spot, having blown their best chance to be champions in a generation.

THE UNLIKELY LADS

On five occasions during the decade, teams went to Wembley and for the first time in their history won a major trophy. If you add on three successive first-timers appearing in FA Cup finals – QPR, Brighton and Watford each losing in their first cup final appearance, from 1982–84 – you might say the eighties were a more meritocratic time; the doors to the trophy cabinets could still be prised open by well-run teams, with a bit of momentum and luck …

1985 Milk Cup Final
Norwich City 1 Sunderland 0

Norwich had more than a bit of history in the League Cup. They had been Second Division winners in a two-legged final against Rochdale back in 1962, and had since lost in two finals in the early 1970s. Sunderland, by contrast, were debuting in the competition's final, but just a dozen years earlier they had turned the football world into a frenzy by upsetting Leeds United in one of the great FA Cup final shocks.

Norwich and Sunderland struggled for most of the 1984/85 season against the threat of relegation, to which they both finally succumbed, and the distraction of a cup run to Wembley was very welcome. As both teams had found goals hard to come by the final seemed unlikely to be goal-fest – and so it proved, with one solitary goal separating the sides. Just moments into the second half, veteran Asa Hartford steered a shot goalwards only for it to be wickedly and decisively deflected off Sunderland's Chisolm, leaving keeper Turner helpless in the Sunderland net. Within minutes Norwich had conceded a penalty, but Sunderland's Clive Walker, probably their biggest threat, fired against a post, and that was the closest Sunderland would come. That year when Norwich finished their league campaign they were eight points clear of lowly Coventry City; unbelievably Coventry went on to win their final three rearranged games and Milk Cup winners Norwich were left with a sour taste in their mouths.

1986 Milk Cup Final
Oxford United 3 QPR 0

Oxford deservedly won their first, and so far only, major trophy with a sparkling attacking display at Wembley against a more fancied Rangers team who were second best all day long. Goals from Hebberd, Houghton and Charles gave United a 3-0 winning margin that did not flatter them; their incisive attacking play was just too much for Rangers.

At the time Oxford were enjoying the most memorable spell in their history, they had gone from Division Three to Division One in two years, going up as champions each year. Manager Jim Smith had overseen the spectacular run, but strangely his contract was not extended by Chairman Robert Maxwell. At the end of the 1985 season Smith took over at QPR, managing them against his old charges in the Wembley final. Oxford's stay in the top flight lasted only three seasons and the intervening time has not been kind to them, years of decline leading to them slipping out the Football League in 2006. Fortunes have turned again recently though, and these days United are back in League One and have made two more recent visits to Wembley as runners-up in the Football League Trophy finals.

1987 FA Cup Final
Coventry City 3 Tottenham Hotspur 2

The Coventry City team of 1987 were a workmanlike team, organised and gritty, but were perceived to be lacking the star quality of their opponents, Tottenham Hotspur. Spurs' line up was a who's who of English football: international star Glenn Hoddle, World Cup winner Ossie Ardiles, forty-eight-goal striker Clive Allen and dazzling wideman Chris Waddle were all names to give Sky Blue fans nightmares.

The final was a thriller for neutrals. Spurs were ahead inside a minute through Clive Allen, and Coventry drew level after ten when Dave Bennett nimbly rounded keeper Clemence to score with a rare left-footed effort. This blistering start set the tone for a match that was dominated by neither team. Instead it ebbed and flowed throughout; the pre-match predictions of Tottenham dominance were certainly wide of the mark.

Spurs nudged ahead after a defensive mix-up led to Gary Mabbutt's goal shortly before half-time, but just after the hour mark Coventry levelled again. Bennett hit the perfect cross, arcing the ball around the full back for striker Houchen to meet it with a spectacular diving header, as good as any seen in a Wembley final. City's extra-time winner came courtesy of a deflected Lloyd McGrath cross; it struck Gary Mabbutt's knee, and in that split second the die was cast. The ball looped up over Clemence and nestled in the far corner of the Tottenham net. For the first time in their 104-year history the Sky Blues had finally won a major trophy.

1988 Littlewoods Cup Final
Luton Town 3 Arsenal 2

When Luton played in this final they were halfway through a ten-year spell in Division One, enjoying the best period in the club's history. The 1988 team was capable of a third consecutive top-ten finish and included some players other teams envied and feared in Mark Stein and Mick Harford. Opponents Arsenal, under George Graham, were emerging as top-six side who had already won the previous year's Littlewoods Cup. They were on the up and were clear favourites for the '88 final.

After thirteen minutes, Luton's Mark Stein opened the scoring, smartly side-footing a through-ball home, and it was a lead they held for almost an hour. With less than twenty minutes remaining, Arsenal hit back with two goals in three minutes to turn the match around. Luton's chances seemed to be slipping away when they then conceded a penalty, but reserve keeper Dibble pulled off another magnificent diving save, this time to his left, and they breathed again. Shortly afterwards, a bouncing ball in the Arsenal penalty area was not dealt with by Gus Ceasar, who famously stumbled as he tried to clear it, allowing Mark Stein to set up Danny Wilson for an equaliser. With the match just seconds from extra-time Luton sub Ashley Grimes crossed first time with the outside of his left foot and that man Stein was there again to steer a volley into Arsenal's net and complete the incredible turnaround.

With little over ten minutes left Luton had trailed 2-1 and faced a penalty against them. They were not so much on the ropes as on the canvas, but thanks to some inspired goalkeeping and smart forward play they had roused themselves to deliver a stunning knockout blow.

1988 FA Cup Final
Wimbledon 1 Liverpool 0

This cup final is often heralded as the ultimate David v. Goliath showdown, and while that might be overstating things a little, as Wimbledon had finished seventh in Division One to Liverpool's first place, the shock the Dons created by winning could have registered on the footballing Richter scale! How the footballing world was turned upside down can be read in more detail elsewhere.

SIMPLY THE BEST

At the 1982 World Cup finals, Brazil manager Telê Santana had a dream-come-true of a team. His list of talented individuals was long: Junior, the free-roaming full back who could appear anywhere; Socrates, the chain-smoking doctor with the deftest of touches, in the middle of the field; Zico, unlocking any defence with more tricks than Paul Daniels, up front. Santana's boys looked expertly equipped to launch the country's first serious attempt at the World Cup since the days of Pelé, Jairzinho and Carlos Alberto.

Brazil's first match against the USSR signposted what they had in their team; trailing 1-0 after a goalkeeping fumble they produced two goals of the highest quality to win. Firstly, Eder hit a firecracker of a volley to level things up after the most insouciant of dummies from Falcao, before Socrates won it with an arrowing shot of such velocity that it might be still travelling if it had not hit the top corner of the Russian net. They were exhibition goals on the highest stage.

Next up were a Scotland team that had a few highly regarded players of their own, with a spine from Liverpool's all-conquering team in Hansen, Souness and Dalglish. The Scots had the cheek to open the scoring with a superb David Narey strike from distance, but this was a bit like waking a sleeping tiger; once Brazil were roused there was only ever one possible outcome. First, Zico's free kick hit the topmost point of Alan Rough's left-hand post, leaving the keeper motionless. Then, Oscar's header followed, before another very special strike, this time Eder chipping the static, suffering Rough to perfection from just inside the left-hand side of the penalty area. A thumping strike from outside the area by Falcao finished the scoring, but in truth this was less of a contest and more of a coronation; on this evidence, against a decent Scottish side, Brazil were playing on another level.

The routine four goal demolition of New Zealand that finished the group matches included two more memorable strikes from Zico – a scissor-kick volley and a calm side-foot after a perfect passing move. Argentina and Italy were up next, but neither had offered anything like the verve and firepower the Brazilians had demonstrated; Santana's men were now not just favourites for the competition, they were favourites for the millions watching around the world and revelling in wave after wave of golden, attacking football.

Argentina were comfortably beaten 3-1: Zico poked in

a rebound from Eder's fierce free-kick, Serginho popped up with a header before the marauding Junior added a sublime third, racing on to Zico's precision pass. Brazil were strong and seemingly getting stronger with each outing. The quality of the goals they were scoring was striking. If Michelangelo's dad had given his teenage prodigy a pair of size 9 pumas instead of a paintbrush, he would surely have scored goals like these – they were skilful, incisive and thrilling; they were masterpieces.

All Brazil had to do was just keep up perfection, but next in line were the masters of spoiling and squeezing, the improving Italians. The *Azzurri* had a chance against anyone, as they had a gunslinger of a forward called Paolo Rossi whose shooting could be deadly. After five minutes it was first strike to Rossi, who nodded home only for the languid Socrates to calmly level soon afterwards – fifteen minutes in and we had a match on our hands.

Ten further minutes were played before what was perhaps the decisive moment of the match occurred: Cerezo's square pass along his back line went straight to Rossi, who advanced, took aim and scored – 2-1 to Italy at half-time. Just after the hour, Falcao benefited from one of the cutest decoy runs you will ever see from Cerezo. In the blink of an eye his dummy run took out three Italian defenders, allowing Falcao to stride forward into into an empty penalty area and shoot powerfully past Zoff, now looking his whole 40 years of age.

Had Brazil only been able to hang on to the 2-2 scoreline, the semi-final berth was theirs. Had they been able to pick up Paolo Rossi, who completed his hat-trick when left unmarked at a corner, things would have been different. But this Brazilian team was a throwback to more light-hearted days, where you just played your game and did not worry too much about the opposition. Brazil's own Achilles heel was the defence that sometimes patrolled behind their magical midfield; what they needed was a scrapper or a stopper, a Scirea, or a Gentile, rugged as the Rockies. Sadly for Brazil, though, there was no such ballast in the defence and the team that thrilled so many were soon packing their suitcases for home. The dream of relentless, carefree attacking football had run aground on the stony rocks of Italian pragmatism. On this occasion, perhaps sadly, the artists were undone by the artisans.

THE THINGS THEY SAY

Lord Nelson, Lord Beaverbrook, Sir Winston Churchill, Sir Anthony Eden, Clement Attlee, Henry Cooper, Lady Diana ... Maggie Thatcher can you hear me? Maggie Thatcher, Your boys took a hell of a beating! Your boys took a hell of a beating!

Bjørge Lillelien

World Cup qualifier, September 1981
Norway 2 England 1
At the sixth time of asking, Norway's part-timers put England's highly fancied stars to the sword in a World Cup qualifier in Oslo in September 1981. As the scale of the home side's achievement became apparent, radio commentator Bjørge Lillelien quickly decided to dispense with the diplomatic niceties and launched into an impressive tirade against as many pillars of the British establishment as he could think of. Lillelien's references ranged from the historical to the contemporary before descending, or maybe ascending, into the downright belligerent and quite memorable 'hell of a beating' line.

DIAMOND GEEZERS

The murky sub-genre of footballers-attempting-to-be-popstars was never a cup that overflowed with obvious talent. The early template of Kevin Keegan's 1979 opus *Head over Heels* had left many fearful of the next time a leading footballer might decide it was time to hit the recording studios and put together a video with visual effects straight out of *Doctor Who* circa 1971.

In April 1987 those fears were found to be fully justified when two of Tottenham's exciting 1987 team, Glenn Hoddle and Chris Waddle, decided it was time to get out the synthesisers and don the three-quarter-length pastel jackets while miming on Top of the Pops. Hoddle and Waddle had enjoyed an outstanding season – getting to the League Cup semi-finals, going on to finish third in Division One and reaching the FA Cup Final too; their reputations were sky-high, they were widely admired as players and, crucially, they had always let their feet do the talking. Until April 1987. Just weeks before the Wembley showpiece with Coventry City, teammates Hoddle and Waddle dropped a musical bombshell called *Diamond Lights* on the unsuspecting public.

The song was not the worst footballer track ever released. It had a recognisable electro beat, one or two swooping crescendos and it even had some lyrics too; indisputably, it was a pop song. As Chris Waddle manfully tried to look like he hadn't been secretly glued to the ground, Glenn Hoddle threw himself into the pop star role with gusto and could have passed for a typical eighties blow-dried pin-up. For certain, reaching no. 12 in the charts adds some credibility to the venture. But the sheer unlikeliness of seeing two talented international footballers pretending to be skilled in a very different area necessitated a certain suspension of disbelief. In short, the would-be crooners were probably better off sticking to their day job, tormenting defenders and creating space, rather than tormenting listeners and creating a racket!

The duo did record a second song, presciently titled 'It's Goodbye', but, so the story goes, the track was never released as Hoddle had signed for Monaco and was handily out of the country. Perhaps Glenn just knew when to stop, though in fairness to them both it is doubtful that the pair were planning on permanently swapping their boots for any more video shoots in *Miami Vice*-style outfits with enigmatic ballerinas any time soon. At one point in *Diamond Lights* Hoddle memorably warbled, 'can't explain, so afraid tonight'; the suspicion lurks that after that *Top of the Pops* appearance he wasn't the only one!

Of course Hoddle had some form not just out on the pitch but in the recording studio too. He had been a part of the England squad that had recorded 'This Time (We'll Get It Right)' for the 1982 World Cup. The obligatory video showcased the players crooning and swooning their way through an afternoon's work at the fabled Abbey Road studios. Just to prove that life is nothing if not in a permanent state of flux, the place where Lennon and McCartney once held court now hosted the doleful tones of Mick Mills and Dave Watson.

Most of the group exuded a cheery demeanour, though Trevor Brooking didn't quite project the required bonhomie; the look on his face suggested a man who was dangerously close to the edge after being forced to listen to 'This Time' on a twelve-hour loop. To be fair to the players, they held themselves together for what was unlikely to have been anyone's first choice for an afternoon out. The video saw everyone kitted out by suppliers Admiral in daring blue and red jerseys, though the effect of this sweater-and-slack-fest was less David Beckham-style fashion icon and more 'Man at C&A'!

To avoid any possible confusion, the lines intoned that that the group was 'Ron's twenty-two' and promised that the players would, 'find a way, find a way to get away, this time'. Sure enough after two goalless second round games, Ron's twenty-two had indeed found a way to get home – simply by not scoring in important games when it mattered most!

THE TEAM THAT JACK BUILT

One-time World Cup winner and proud Englishman Jack Charlton was not everyone's choice for Republic of Ireland manager in early 1986, but after a decade in charge there were very few Irish fans who would not acknowledge the monumental role he had played in developing the national side from perennial also-rans to regular qualifiers for major competitions.

When Charlton was initially shortlisted for the job, the FAI had an election process to go through and in the first round of voting Charlton did not secure the highest number of votes, ex-Liverpool boss Bob Paisley did. As the voting went on and other names dropped out, Charlton's chances improved, and when some changed their allegiances away from Paisley, the job was Charlton's. At the time the announcement was made, in the days before mobiles, Charlton was away and uncontactable, already displaying a stubborn and independent streak.

At the time of the new appointment, Ireland undoubtedly had talented players: O'Leary, McGrath, Whelan and an ageing Liam Brady were all players of the highest pedigree, yet somehow qualification for major finals had always eluded them. Charlton did not take long to see what he needed to alter – and the changes were immediate. He wanted the players to enjoy their international breaks much more, so any previous splintering of the squad into separate groups had to stop. Players were to be more involved with each other, socially as well as professionally, because the new manager wanted a closely bonded group of players, a bit like a club style, and soon he got it.

Before his first game, an unpromising 1-0 home defeat at home to Wales, Charlton had also started work on increasing his pool of potential players. He contacted clubs, asking them to let it be known that he wanted players who qualified

for Ireland through their family backgrounds. Straight away
Oxford United's John Aldridge came into the fold, through
grand-maternal lineage, and when Aldridge told Charlton that
teammate Ray Houghton had an Irish father, Charlton had
two players for the price of one. Both started that first match
against Wales and went on to be major players for a decade.

Ireland were sometimes heavily criticised for this courting
and capturing of players from an Irish line of descent. The
'plastic paddies' label was thrown at the likes of Hughton,
Houghton, McCarthy and Sheedy. In reality, though, all
Charlton and Ireland did was use the same rules that were
there for all international teams, and as Ireland had suffered
more than most nations from emigration over the centuries,
the fact that the Irish football team benefited from their own
wide diaspora had a certain symmetry to it.

Charlton's first target was qualifying for Euro '88, and
though the goals did not flow, with just ten scored in eight
games, the results were good: four wins, three draws and only
one reverse in the whole campaign. The group was close –
only two points would finally separate Ireland, Belgium,
Bulgaria and Scotland – but it was Ireland who, for the first
time in their history, came out on top. The decisive moment
came when Scotland's Gary Mackay scored a late winner
against Bulgaria to deny the home side and send Charlton
and his team to Germany for the finals. Reaction at home
was phenomenal, with interest in the national team surging as
Euro fever broke out in all areas.

Possibly Charlton's finest moment as manager came in the
team's first ever game in the finals of a major tournament,
when Ireland played and beat England 1-0 in Stuttgart. An
early Ray Houghton goal, a looping header after a defensive
mix-up, settled the game, but not before all kinds of drama
was played out. Packie Bonner in the Ireland goal played one
of the matches of his life to repel everything that England,
and Gary Lineker in particular, fired at him; Lineker was very
much out-of-form in front of goal, while Bonner played

out-of-his-skin. Ireland followed that up with the better of a 1-1 draw with the Soviet Union, which left them needing to avoid defeat against highly regarded Holland to, unbelievably, reach the last four of the competition. Charlton's men came agonisingly close; they were eight minutes from the semi-final when a slightly fortuitous Wim Kieft header span at an unlikely angle into Bonner's net.

Charlton's men went home as heroes and they could do little wrong in the eyes of their adoring fans. The team was not immune to criticism from some quarters though, with one or two pundits in particular emphasising their direct style of play and the paucity of the football they played. For sure, Charlton was no idealist when it came to winning football matches; there were to be no aesthetically pleasing passing triangles nor any attempt at a possession-based style to gradually wear teams down in an early forerunner of Spain's tiki-taka. Instead Charlton was pragmatic in almost everything he got his teams to do. Ireland had a clear style and game plan, and crucially the players mastered their brief and stuck to it. Simply put, Ireland would press high up the pitch to be handily placed when they regained the ball. They did not pass through the midfield and they hit their forwards early with long balls. Charlton did not deliver football for the purist, but he did deliver results for the team and their fans. Although within that set-up were some high-class players – Whelan, McGrath and Houghton immediately spring to mind – Ireland did not have an abundance of stellar names to choose from in each position. Some say Charlton should have adopted a more expansive style, but it remains a fact that his results were spectacular and this was largely because, like the best managers always do, he used what he had to maximum effect.

MOMENT IN TIME: RICKY VILLA, 1981

When Tottenham won the FA Cup in 1981, it was still a time when the cup mattered enormously. Those pre-satellite days meant football fans were strictly rationed to a meagre diet of live matches: no league games. Occasional internationals and cup finals were your lot. For a cup final to throw up drama, goals of the highest quality and a winning strike that could have graced any stage, anywhere, meant you had hit a footballing jackpot – and that is exactly what the FA Cup Final of 1981 was.

Tottenham Hotspur and Manchester City had shared a 1-1 draw on the Saturday afternoon; it was an interesting, but hardly thrilling encounter, and the portents for the replay were not auspicious. Happily, the match was a cracker, lit up by two teams going at full pelt and with some considerable attacking verve on display. The first four goals were shared, Villa nudging Spurs ahead early on before City fought back to lead 2-1 with Mackenzie's sublime volley a highlight, only for Garth Crooks to sharply level the score for Spurs.

With less than fifteen minutes left and the sides locked at 2-2, calling a winner was difficult; the usual factors of someone slipping up or someone stepping up were looking the most likely way to decide an evenly contested final. On this occasion, it was the latter, and it was Spurs' Ricky Villa, forlornly substituted in the first match, who was to etch himself a place in cup final folklore.

When Villa received the ball close to 30 yards from the City goal, he had five blue City shirts between him and Joe Corrigan; the way he set off, though, there could have been ten defenders there and they might not have been able to stop him. Vila ran straight at the tired legs of City defenders Caton and Ranson, effortlessly dribbling past them, one way and then the other.

In the slaloming style that Lionel Messi has made his trademark in recent years, Villa simply toyed with his opponents. Like a dad guesting in an under-10s game, the Spurs number five had far too many tricks for his opponents, and as City's Corrigan came out to meet him the ball was slid home for a winning goal of the deftest skill and highest quality. The image of the bearded Argentinian resplendent in his shiny Le Coq Sportif shirt leaving opponents floored behind him became a defining FA Cup moment.

SNAKES AND LADDERS

One of the best things about watching any sport should be its complete unpredictability; it's why we keep tuning in and turning up. The following clubs had both unbearable and unbelievable runs which would have been impossible to predict, leaving spectators to sit back and watch the unlikely and the improbable unfold.

When Bristol City were promoted to the First Division in 1976 there was plenty of room for optimism around Ashton Gate; the team was on the up, and within a year they had won the Anglo-Scottish Cup. As the 1980s began, though, the Robins were soon unravelling as they were hit by three successive relegations, taking them from away trips to Manchester United in 1980 to Rochdale by 1982. The fall was made complicated by financial difficulties that left the club in danger of folding at one point. Though the fall was swift, the climb back up the leagues was anything but. They finished the eighties still in the third tier – looking upwards, but from a distance.

Anything Bristol City could do, it seemed, Wolves could do just as well, as they repeated the three-year fall down the leagues. Wolves managed to go from top to bottom divisions in successive years after being relegated in 1984, 1985 and finally in 1986. Fans did not have too long to wait for a turnaround in their fortunes, however, as they were Division Four and Division Three champions in successive years and won a Football League Trophy final too. The combination of Steve Bull and Andy Mutch did a lot to revive the club, and they became a high-scoring team once more, with their eyes on better days.

In their first season in the top flight, 1981/82, Swansea City looked like they had found their rightful place; a sixth-place finish rewarded some bright attacking performances under

John Toshack, and the Swans were making friends and gaining admirers. Yet within four years they went from top flight to basement and a decade-long period away from football's elite beckoned.

People say that for every ying there is a yang, and so it was that while Wolves, Swansea and Bristol City were busy going through the leagues like the proverbial dose of salts there were other teams travelling, at some speed, in the exact opposite direction. Oxford United won successive promotions as champions of Division Three and Division Two under Jim Smith's shrewd leadership to take their place in Division One. In their first season in the top flight they also celebrated a Wembley win in the League Cup Final, but within three seasons they were to embark on a downward spiral which would eventually see them drop out of the Football League altogether for a time.

Wimbledon is probably the most quoted example of an upwardly mobile team; they astonishingly went from non-league to Football League, to Division One, to FA Cup winners within ten years. Still plying their trade in Division Four in the 1982/83 season, it took the Dons only four years to achieve three promotions. Their winning combination was based around manager Dave Bassett's pragmatic tactics, an irrepressible team spirit and a certain ruggedness in their approach. They can be sometimes overlooked given the headline names of Vinnie Jones and John Fashanu on the team sheets, but Wimbledon did have one or two players who could play a bit too – Dennis Wise and Terry Gibson certainly did not rely on brawn to get by. When they arrived in the top flight though, the Dons did not look out of place finishing sixth and then seventh in their first two years up. If you throw in an FA Cup Final win against Liverpool for good measure, their ascent up the leagues was incredible, making their subsequent decline, relocation and finally rise back from footballing oblivion even more poignant.

RED LETTER DAYS

2 SEPTEMBER 1980 saw First Division Southampton travel to Second Division Watford for what should have been fairly routine League Cup second round, second leg. The Saints had a 4-0 lead from the first leg and there was nothing from that outing to suggest Watford were anything but dead and buried in the tie.

Graham Taylor's men faced a Kevin Keegan-less Southampton team, but the Saints still had quality throughout their ranks – England internationals Dave Watson, Charlie George and Mick Channon provided the knowhow while Steve Williams and Nick Holmes the legs.

Perhaps Southampton turned up thinking, not unreasonably, that the job was done, but for whatever reason they simply fell to pieces under Watford's bombardment. Two first half Watford goals made things interesting and when a third followed in the second period the tie was alive again. Shortly after though an own goal by Steve Sims seemed to have ended the contest, only for Watford's goals to keep on flowing. By ninety minutes the aggregate score was 5-5 and in the extra half-hour Taylor's men added two more to complete a 7-1 win on the night and a 7-5 aggregate win in a turnaround seldom seen in cup football.

———————

11 JULY 1982 was the day that Italy secured their third World Cup triumph, defeating West Germany 3-1; it was also the day that goalkeeper Dino Zoff struck a blow for the middle-aged everywhere by becoming the oldest player to win the World Cup, aged 40. Some fourteen years after making his debut for the *Azzurri*, Zoff continued to excel at what was, for any professional footballer, an advanced age, and he was voted the best goalkeeper in the finals.

That Italian vintage simply got better and better with every game, but they are perhaps best remembered for the thrilling 3-2 win over Brazil's expansive side. With just moments to go and his side defending their narrow lead, Zoff produced one of his most important and probably finest saves for his country. Eder's free kick from the left was powerfully met by a downward header by Oscar. Zoff was at full stretch and got both hands to the ball only for it to agonisingly squirm out of his hands, perhaps two inches from the goal-line. Before the ball could trickle over to equalise for Brazil, Zoff somehow reached out and extended his arms to stop the ball on the goal-line itself, once again displaying fantastic athleticism and immaculate timing – not bad for an old-timer!

---

11 MAY 1983 will forever be remembered fondly by Aberdeen fans as the day their heroes made the impossible possible. It was the day they met and beat Real Madrid in a European final.

Under Alex Ferguson's leadership the Dons were a club transformed. He had already brought them domestic success with both a Scottish title and a couple of Scottish Cups, and now his charges had reached their first European final in Gothenberg to play Madrid for the European Cup Winners Cup. The Aberdeen team had some established names of the Scottish game: keeper Leighton was protected by defensive pillars McLeish and Miller, while further up the field the craft of Strachan was allied to the goal threat of McGhee and Black. But while they were no pushover, they were certainly the underdogs.

Despite the deluge, Aberdeen started promisingly and within ten minutes Eric Black had turned a corner in to open the scoring. Shortly afterwards a horror of a back-pass from McLeish allowed Madrid's Santillana through, only for him to be upended by Leighton and the penalty was converted. As the match wore on the teams appeared evenly matched and it was hard to pick a winner. Debuting in their first European final, Aberdeen had played above most people's expectations; Madrid, the side with six European Cup triumphs stacked away, had not made their experience count, and the game went into an extra half-hour. With the prospect of penalties getting ever closer, substitute Hewitt's glancing header from McGhee's cross proved to be the winner for the Dons. A late onslaught from Real was withstood and the riotous celebrations began; the streets of Gothenberg and Aberdeen alike were filled with delirious Dons fans.

Many had made their way to Sweden on the *St Clair*, and the nearly two days the ferry took for the return journey was merrily alcohol-fuelled as fans simply partied. If the result was a fantastic surprise for the Dons' fans, they soon had another surprise waiting on the quayside when manager Ferguson arrived, trophy in hand, to greet the alcohol-weary fans ashore. Under Ferguson's stewardship they had taken their seat at the top table of European football and did not look out of place for a minute.

---

14 MAY 1983 marked the end of one of English football's greatest-ever managerial spells when Liverpool's Bob Paisley retired after nine years at the helm. In his time as manager Paisley won three European Cups, a UEFA Cup, six League titles, three League Cups, six Charity Shields and one European Super Cup. He had averaged nearly two major trophies a year for a decade – despite having never wanted the job in the first place! He is one of only three men – Carlo Ancelotti and Zinedine Zidane are the others – who have won three European Cups; as glittering CVs go, Paisley's outshines just about every other manager's.

Paisley progressed through the ranks at Anfield, working in almost every role on the football side: first he was a player for fifteen years (six were lost to the war); he followed that by becoming a coach, then a physio and latterly a trusted assistant to Bill Shankly before finally coming into his own as the manager of the club. Nobody knew Liverpool better and nobody did more for the club.

Paisley's ability to spot a player – he didn't seem to sign too many bad ones – was a major strength, and stories from within Anfield tell of a straight-talking manager whose toughness belied his avuncular appearance; the homely jumpers were deceptive! Paisley also liked to keep things simple. Not for him was the detailed dossier approach to opponents. He preferred instead to tell his players not to complicate things, just to go out and play – which was exactly what they did to great effect.

---

26 MAY 1984 witnessed the last ever match in the Home International Championships, as England and Scotland played out a 1-1 draw at Hampden Park. As neither side could force a victory the draw allowed Northern Ireland to finish as the final winners of the championship.

The competition had been running for 100 years and for most of that time had been an eagerly awaited end of season jamboree; the local rivalries were both fierce and friendly, with the smaller nations enjoying the chance to bloody the noses of their supposedly more illustrious neighbours. However the championships had been in marked decline in recent years; attendances were dropping, and since 1981's cancelled competition there were genuine security fears regarding travel in Northern Ireland. To have maintained spectator's interest and enthusiasm for a whole 100 years took some doing, but when the annual fixtures stopped there were not many dissenting voices; it was time for the home nations to look further afield for more rigorous tests.

BULL

For any striker to score 306 times in their career is a magnificent achievement, guaranteeing entry into a very elite band of strikers. To do so for one club is simply staggering, the stuff of club legends. That pretty much describes Wolverhampton Wanderers' burly, deadly number nine, Steve Bull.

After being spotted scoring regularly at his local club, Tipton Town, Bull was taken to West Bromwich Albion. At The Hawthorns, the goals continued in the Baggies' reserve team, and though he did score a couple in the first team, his outings with them were limited. Albion boss Ron Saunders agreed to let local rivals Wolves snap the player up for a £50,000 transfer fee. Bull proved to be a snip at the price.

In his first season at Wolves, Bull settled nicely into Division Four, scoring almost twenty goals. But that was only the warm-up act. In the next two years he netted over fifty times in each year, propelling Wolves to successive Fourth and Third Division championships with a Football League Trophy win at Wembley for good measure. Bull was consistently excelling at the strongest part of his game – he was simply a superb goal-scorer. He had some pace, he had a bucketful of enthusiasm and energy, but more than anything he could shoot with power and precision.

Bull's headlining act in the lower leagues became harder and harder to ignore, and in May 1989, when still technically a Third Division player, he was called up to the England senior squad; he is still the last player to play for England from outside of the top two tiers. While doubts about his touch and finesse persisted, no one could doubt the power with which he could whack a ball into a net, because he did exactly that against Scotland at Hampden Park to seal a debut goal in a 2-0 England win. Bull was highly enough thought of for Bobby Robson to take him as a goal-scoring option from the substitute's bench to Italia '90, and he made four appearances on football's highest stage.

It is at Molineux, though, where Bull is most revered; his longevity, his loyalty and his love of trying to burst the net in Wolves' famous old gold shirt ensured enduring affection for Tipton's finest. Perhaps Bullseye host Jim Bowen might have had his eye on more than just his prize dartboard when he regularly told us, 'you can't beat a bit of bully!'

FLICK TO KICK

As the 1980s kicked off, both the footballing and real worlds were very different places to the ones we inhabit today. One reading of those pre-internet, pre-satellite TV and pre-premiership days can be that they were simpler, more innocent times, though the prevalence of football-related disorder might disprove that rosy theory. For sure, though, we can say without too much fear of contradiction that the eighties were very different days – so different, in fact, that millions of football fans got their kicks far from the terraces, upon green baize rectangles filled with wobbly plastic figures. Like new wave music and leg warmers, the world of Subbuteo began the decade booming.

The tabletop football game, which Peter Adolph had first developed shortly after the war, was simplicity itself. Mini-football figures on wobbly bases were flicked from one end of a pitch to another, as diving goalkeepers attempted to keep disproportionately huge balls out of their nets. Subbuteo had action, it had competition and it had everything the football nut could possibly desire. There was a set of players to practise formations with, convincing team colours, and even replica trophies to raise in triumph. There were goalposts and nets, perimeter fences with adverts, scoreboards, corner flags, and even corner takers – enough paraphernalia to satisfy both the casual player and the niche obsessive. For the younger player the creation of your own parallel universe afforded you the kind of football omnipotence usually only enjoyed by Jimmy Hill; for the older enthusiast there were many local leagues to test out your flicking fingers.

The reported number of players worldwide peaked at 7,000,000 in 1982, representing an all-time high point for the game. Its enduring appeal was emphasised in 1987 when, sixteen years after first achieving the feat, Subbuteo was once again named the prestigious Toy of the Year.

At that point it seemed likely to stay around for decades to come. It was at just about that same time, though, that many of the nation's teenage heads were being turned away from their own plastic reality to a new screen-based, virtual one, as home computers began their inexorable march. Vic-20s, Commodore 64s and the Sinclair ZX-81 started a shift towards more visual, and eventually immersive games that would, in time, render Subbuteo slow and static by comparison.

In the same way music lovers of a certain vintage champion vinyl over digital downloads, so it is that Subbuteo players of an earlier era can often scoff at the antics of Alex Hunter on their children's bionically-detailed FIFA '17 games. Of course, comparisons between games of different eras, as between players from different decades, are fun but impossible to prove. However, it might just be that Subbuteo does have the edge in one key area. Arguably, until the FIFA aficionados can match Feargal Sharkey's warbling lament, on The Undertones' 1980 top-ten hit 'My Perfect Cousin' – when cousin Kevin famously 'flicked to kick' but Feargal didn't know – with a genius pop couplet of their own, the latest score remains Subbuteo 1 FIFA 0!

CELEBRATIONS

Supporters young and old like nothing better than seeing a memorable goal adorned with an even more memorable celebration, and here are some of the finest of the decade:

David Pleat, Luton Town manager
Maine Road, May 1983

After winning plenty of friends, but not quite enough points, Luton Town faced a relegation showdown at fellow strugglers Manchester City in the final game of the 1982/83 season. City had been in freefall since Christmas, but needed only a point to secure their survival, while nothing less than victory would see David Pleat's men safe.

After eighty-five goalless minutes the odds were heavily stacked in City's favour, until Luton broke down the right and City keeper Alex Williams unconvincingly palmed a cross out to the edge of his penalty area. The ball dropped to future Real Madrid manager Raddy Antić, who, without breaking stride, powered the ball into the bottom corner of Williams's net.

When Luton's safety was secured and City's relegation confirmed just five minutes later, David Pleat simply combusted with joy. He went careering across the touchline, and, in scenes of unadulterated joy, freewheeled across the Maine Road pitch with arms aloft, stopping only to adjust his suit buttons. Resembling a latter-day hurdling Bilbo Baggins, the tightly curled master tactician was a blur of beige as he raced across the grass, inadvertently trampling on the broken hearts of over 40,000 City fans. As they had notched sixty-five league goals but conceded a monumental eighty-four, few begrudged Pleat and his exciting team another season in the First Division.

Marco Tardelli, Italian international
The Bernabéu Stadium, July 1982

The 1982 World Cup in Spain is rightly remembered for many things: for the splendour of Brazil's best-team-to-never-win-the-World-Cup; for Harald Schumacher's assault on Patrick Battiston; and perhaps most of all for Marco Tardelli's goal celebration in the final against West Germany.

In an era when challenges really did crunch, Tardelli was a robust, tough-tackling, defensively-minded midfielder. Crucially, he could also play, and represented both Juventus and Italy for the best part of a decade. During the 1982 World Cup, fuelled by Paolo Rossi's goals, After spluttering through their group with only three draws, the Italians revved up against Brazil and Poland to reach their fourth World Cup Final, this time against West Germany. Momentum was with the *Azzurri* as they set about dismantling the Germans, with some bright, incisive forward play. With Italy already leading through Rossi's stooping header, just after the hour sweeper Gaetano Scirea broke up a German attack and led a swift counter-attack. In the style of a chess grandmaster toying with an opponent, Italy soon found holes in the German defence. When the ball was played back to Tardelli on the edge of the penalty area, the midfielder took a touch with his left before rapidly firing home for a goal of the highest quality.

While Tardelli's goal was excellent, it was the next few seconds that would etch themselves into Italian consciousness. With his arms pumping like locomotive pistons, head shaking wildly in a kind of manic delirium and screaming mouth as wide open as the German defence, for those few seconds Tardelli transcended football and offered the millions of viewers the rawest of emotions, the purest joy. In Italy the celebration was christened *L'urlo di Tardelli* – the Tardelli Scream – and it took on a cultural life of its own, a bit like Gazza's tears at Italia '90, but with a winner's medal. Tardelli later remarked on the immense joy of scoring and how he had been born with that scream inside of him; it seems that as well of a hell of a shot he had a neat line in poetry too!

DAVID v. GOLIATH: SUTTON UNITED 2 COVENTRY CITY 1, 1989

In January 1989 a classic FA Cup Third Round tie saw Coventry City, who were fourth in Division One, travel to Sutton United, then sitting thirteenth in the fifth tier Vauxhall Conference. Little less than eighteen months before, Coventry had beaten Spurs to win the 1987 FA Cup Final, and the Sky Blues were now threatening to become a regular top-ten, top-flight outfit. In fact, just days before the trip to Gander Green Lane, Coventry had demolished Sheffield Wednesday 5-0 and were in robust shape. Sutton, by contrast, were scratching around the lower reaches of the Conference and had shown no signs of being able to engineer any kind of cup shock; an away win was very much on the cards.

Sometimes, of course, a rare combination of chance or circumstances can align and create havoc; if you throw together a muddy pitch, the *Match of the Day* cameras, a little dollop of good fortune and a mildly eccentric manager you might just have all the ingredients for a shock of seismic proportions.

It is certainly possible that Coventry's players felt uncomfortable in their more modest surroundings, and it is undeniable that the occasion, the crowd and the cameras would have all helped the adrenaline flow more quickly through the Sutton player's veins. However, the idea of good fortune can be overstated for Sutton, as at times they out played the Sky Blues and could have scored more. Two smartly-taken set-piece goals, from Tony Rains and Matthew Hanlan, suggested that English literature teacher and manager Barrie Williams had schooled his players well; their drills were played to perfection. Coventry had been statuesque in their defending and did not seem to realise the peril they were facing until too late into the second half.

In the final half-hour City woke up and chased the game. England international Regis was an inch away from equalising, while Wembley hero Houchen hit the bar; the Sky Blues even rattled both bar and post within seconds, but Sutton held on for the sweetest of victories.

Manager Barry Williams enjoyed some fleeting fame of his own as he eschewed any semblance of manager-speak, preferring to quote the words of Rudyard Kipling in the programme notes:

It ain't the individual
Nor the Army as a whole
It's the everlasting team work
Of every bloomin' soul.

On that occasion, of course, the teacher was right; what he said after their 8-0 reverse at Norwich City in the next round, how-ever, remains unprintable!

TOP OF THE WORLD

When the Football Association celebrations for their 100th year were being planned, the showpiece occasion was a match between the Football League and the Rest of the World. Considering that at the time English teams were still banned from European competitions post–Heysel, and that the national team had not gone beyond a quarter-final for over twenty years, it could have been an occasion filled with egg on faces – but it turned out to be anything but.

In the warm-up the world's best player, Diego Maradona, drew gasps from crowd and opposing players alike when he launched the ball almost into orbit before repeatedly trapping the ball immaculately with the deftest of touches. The scourge of England just twelve months before in the Mexico World Cup, resembled an adult in a junior school kick-about – way ahead of the opposition.

A cursory list of the Football League team did not inspire immediate confidence, with Chelsea's Steve Clarke and Watford's John McClelland among the lesser luminaries shoring up a defence which the twinkle-toed Platini and Maradona were expected to dance through. However, no match was ever decided on the team sheet alone, and the Football League boys put in what is best described as a shift. They were more physical, quicker to the ball, and in goalscorers Bryan Robson and Norman Whiteside they had the best performers on the pitch. Though common consent had it that Maradona was the world's best player, it was Robson who gave the masterclass of attacking midfield play. His two goals were typical of the player: a perfectly-timed thumping far-post header was coupled with a characteristic forward burst and first-time finish.

While the whole occasion had the air of a pre-season friendly or even testimonial about it, the afternoon was not entirely friendly. Maradona's every touch was remorselessly booed by a crowd not yet willing to move on from his controversial dismantling of England twelve months before; Diego himself seemed happy enough to trouser a large cheque, reportedly a whopping £100,000, as he played the role of villain to perfection.

AGAINST ALL ODDS

Shortly before hosting Europa 1980, Italian football found itself mired in an unsavoury mix of deception and double-dealings as a ruinous match-fixing scandal, *totonero,* emerged. The integrity of the game in both Serie A and B was called into question when it was discovered that some leading players had been bribed to fix the outcome of matches.

In Italy at the time, the state monopoly on gambling, *Totocalcio*, allowed no betting on individual games – a bit like the football pools in England. It was viewed as a trustworthy way to have a flutter. Unfortunately though, the prospect of rigging games for larger rewards proved too much for some to resist, and a syndicate aiming to fix scores in Serie A and B grew. The scam was discovered – but the trail went far beyond the two businessmen in Rome who were attempting to secure certain scores.

In March 1980, Italian police swooped on grounds across the country and eleven players were immediately arrested on suspicion of match-fixing. That individual players were incriminated was damaging enough, but before long some clubs, major ones too, were being asked some very difficult questions.

As the investigation dug deeper and deeper, AC Milan and Lazio were found to have been involved and were both relegated, while half a dozen other clubs were docked points for the following season. The crisis went deep into Italian football and as it ran its course the highest-profile player to be implicated was Perugia's Paolo Rossi, then a highly regarded young striker who had already enjoyed an outstanding World Cup in 1978.

Rossi received one of the longer bans handed out, of three years, which would have resulted in him missing the next World Cup. The length of his ban was reduced to enable him to play a handful of matches, by then for Juventus, just before the '82 finals. History records that Rossi went on to enjoy the purplest of patches in Spain, hitting six goals as he took home both the Golden Boot and a World Cup winner's medal. Even long after the dust settled on the whole sorry affair, Rossi continued to deny his role in *totonero*, but what could not be denied was his outstanding striking ability; when the ball fell to him inside any penalty area, you would bet your life on him scoring.

THE BAD OLD DAYS

The experience of attending football matches in the eighties was a very different one to that enjoyed by contemporary spectators. The most obvious changes immediately spring to mind – the terraces have gone, tickets are now much more expensive and there is no longer a sprinkling of foreign-based players – more like a galaxy of them. Football has certainly changed and the business of watching football has changed enormously too.

Before the Hillsborough disaster and the subsequent *Taylor Report*, almost all grounds had terraced areas. These varied in location and size, but mostly the more vociferous home fans would form their home end behind one goal, and after warmly welcoming opposition fans to the stadium with ditties such as 'after the match you're gonna die', large parts of the afternoon would be taken up by loudly exhorting their team to score!

The experience of being part of the event was more keenly felt on the terraces, as physically you were that much more involved. In a crowd you might sway along with the anthemic chants and you could swoop with each near miss or goal; in a crowd you could also feel the breathless crush of a squash as your feet left the ground and you were carried yards, or tens of yards, down the steeply banked rows of concrete. All at once the terraces could be exciting, atmospheric and even intoxicating – not everyone's cup of tea, for sure, but for younger and louder fans, they were perfect. Compare the terraces with today's mostly covered, spacious, often newly-built, or even redeveloped stadiums. Today there is more comfort – when it rains you can now usually escape the obligatory eighties drenching – but, as many suggest, perhaps some atmosphere had been lost. The idea of safe standing areas is mooted from time to time, and it may be that it is not beyond the wit of man to devise controlled and safe open areas sometime in the future.

At the end of the 1980s football had not fully tapped into its financial potential, but in the intervening decades it certainly has got the hang of all things commercial. The steep price hikes in match-day tickets is the most glaring example of the way for clubs now maximise their revenue streams from spectators – or if you prefer, milk the fans for everything they've got. At the end of the 1980s to pay more than a fiver for top-flight football would have been rare, yet these days the average price of a Premier League ticket is nudging close to £40, despite the latest TV deal benefiting clubs by a minimum of £100 million! You don't need to be a maths teacher to spot that ticket prices have risen close to 800 per cent, while wages …

Back in the eighties, foreign players were a bit like oranges used to be; in the days before you could a buy a bag of them for a couple of quid they had a certain rarity value and a certain sense of the exotic, simply because there weren't too many of them around. First Tottenham, with Villa and

Ardiles, and then Ipswich with Muhren and Thijssen, were the trailblazers with successful foreign imports. By the end of the decade the slow dribble of foreign talent had probably progressed to something like a trickle, but the British game remained resolutely British; it would take the advent of satellite TV and its attendant big bucks to accelerate the flow of gifted, and sometimes less-gifted, European players into the highways and byways of Divisions One to Four. Very different ways in very different days.

OPENING THE FLOODGATES

In October 1983, when Tottenham Hotspur became the first professional football club to be listed on the stock market, the move heralded a very different approach to club ownership which persists to this day. A statement released at the time summed up the directors' thinking behind the move succinctly: '... will seek to increase the group's income by improving the return from existing assets and by establishing new sources of revenue in the leisure field'.

A very different style of ownership was on the way. The days of football clubs existing primarily for the provision of sport for a local community were not over, but they were changing. For almost 100 years prior to this, football clubs made or lost their money pretty much in proportion to their success on the field and the attendances they could attract. More fortunate clubs would be patronised, even bankrolled, by benevolent benefactors, often locals who made good and wanted to put something back into their community, almost as a kind of a public service. For sure, many club owners may have enjoyed a perk or two on the back of their involvement with the local club, but the basic premise that football clubs were not commercial vehicles to be traded about had held sway for decades until

Tottenham's floatation. That stock market move became, in effect, football's first tentative steps away from being sport-orientated organisations and towards a very different, business-led model of ownership. The FA had foreseen such a possibility, and their Rule 34 was specifically crafted to protect the game from commercialism, and yet Spurs chairman was Alan Sugar was able to simply dance around it by creating a new holding company, Tottenham Hotspur PLC, which then listed the club as a subsidiary of it.

Once it was seen as a success, many more clubs followed Tottenham's lead and became PLCs. Some argued that the effect was to turn football from the sport it had been for almost 100 years into just another business, this time within the entertainment sector. Whether people sided with that analysis or not, it was hard to deny that the days of supporters being seen as fans were certainly changing; they became a 'captive market' whom club owners could always rely upon to keep turning up to consume the product on offer, however much ticket prices were hiked up.

The roots of the Premier League could in part be traced back to these early moves at White Hart Lane, but one other hugely significant financial change in the eighties did just as much to open the floodgates to speculative owners seeking to max out their client bases. In 1988 the decades-long practice of both teams getting a share from the gate receipts was stopped. Critics suggested this move was unfair and could only undermine and erode the great competitive framework of the Football League, in which teams of different sizes and stature could compete. To prove the point, the start of the eighties had seen teams of limited resources like Southampton and Watford finishing second in the old First Division. These were days when you might not have been able to predict the top four teams in the league before each season began with a tedious, unerring accuracy. However, once gate receipts were kept by home teams only, it simply meant that the bigger teams with the bigger crowds got to have even bigger bank balances too – which very nearly takes us to the pre-eminence and domination of Manchester United throughout the 1990s!

The combination of the floating of clubs on the stock market and of more clubs having the ability to retain their own gate receipts meant that by the end of the eighties the gates to previously undreamt of financial possibilities had been opened, and they were not about to be closed. The commercial juggernaut that is modern football, replete with its many leisure and lifestyle brands to select from, was rumbling ever closer.

THE THINGS THEY SAY

It's come straight out to Socrates. Socrates still. Trying to get the opening. Oh Socrates! Whoa, what a goal
                                                    John Helm, ITV

World Cup group match, June 1982
Brazil 2 USSR 1
For sheer boyish enthusiasm, John Helm's awestruck lines accompanying Socrates' equalising strike are hard to beat. Like the footballing god that he was, Socrates aimed his strike to perfection, leaving millions watching worldwide with just about the only possible response – 'whoa, what a goal!'

BARNES

John Barnes began the decade as an athletic and talented youth player for Stowe Boys Club in London, and he ended it as one of the most revered players in the country, starring for both Liverpool and England. The journey Barnes made from middle-class Jamaica, the son of an army Colonel, to high-class footballer was not your average young-kid-makes-the-grade story, there was little about Barnes, in his background or his game, that was ever average.

Arriving in England from Jamaica as a sporty 13-year-old, Barnes enjoyed his time with Stowe, and when youth football ended he progressed to men's football with Sudbury Court, many leagues below the Conference in the Middlesex League Premier Division. It was a step up to proper, competitive men's football and Barnes' talent, then displayed on the right side of midfield, shone through as the team won their league convincingly. By now Barnes was being looked at by professional clubs, and after a taxi driver alerted Graham Taylor's Watford, the professional game beckoned.

Six successful years at Vicarage Road followed for Barnes in what was a golden time for Watford. Promotion to Division One, an FA Cup Final appearance and a runners-up slot in the league were all accomplished under Graham Taylor's careful tutelage as Barnes' star continued to rise. In the middle of this time at Watford, Barnes also hit one of the highest points of his England career, with a superb, slalomed dribble of a goal against Brazil at the Maracana Stadium; for those few seconds the 20-year-old Barnes played like Maradona in his pomp – it was stunning stuff.

Thousands of miles from home, though, on that same South American tour, some of English society's worst traits came to the fore on a plane trip Barnes and his teammates took to Chile. As a black player in predominantly white England, Barnes had become familiar with, perhaps even hardened to, the appalling racist abuse that could still cascade from the terraces, but what Barnes heard on the flight seemed to plumb new depths. National Front supporters sitting towards the back of the plane repeatedly said of England's 2-0 win in the Maracana that they had 'only won 1-0'; the wonder goal scored by Barnes did not count in their racist eyes because he was black.

Although England and English football grounds would eventually begin to change for the better, it is worth remembering that this incident was still nine years before even the flagship anti-racist organisation *Kick it Out* was formed; there was simply a very long way to go to alter attitudes and expectations. For Barnes and his contemporaries, the progress in reducing racism could feel painfully slow.

The summer of 1987 brought Barnes a big-money move to Liverpool, and there he flourished. Anfield was the perfect place for Barnes to showcase his talents; immediately he played with pace and purpose, and seemingly with glue on his boots at times, in an exciting Liverpool team used to winning. Early league titles and later cup wins were added to by a host of individual honours: Barnes picked up a Players' Player of the Year and two Football Writers' Footballer of the awards.

With England, as sometimes has been the case for leading club men, things were not so spectacular. Although Barnes was a key part of several successful qualifying campaigns and he played in two World Cups and a Euro finals, he never dazzled on the international stage in quite the same way that he did at Anfield. Perhaps playing with better, certainly more dominant, teams at Liverpool made life easier for Barnes in a red Liverpool shirt than in the white of England, but his relatively modest international career should not detract from his achievements.

At his best, before an Achilles injury reduced his pace, Barnes was as close to unplayable as you get to see every generation; he out-muscled, he out-moved and he out-skilled opponents. A bit like a dad joining in in a kid's playground kick-about, he was just better than everyone else!

BROKEN HEARTS

Until the 1980s added some much-needed interest to proceedings, the Scottish championship had become a two-horse race for the best part of two decades. Only once in seventeen years had a champion come from outside of the prevailing duopoly of Glasgow Rangers and Glasgow Celtic. If ever a league needed some competitive freshening up it was the Scottish Premier League as the 1980s emerged.

The good news for Scottish football fans was that not just one, but two other clubs were now able to sustain a challenge to the Old Firm as Alex Ferguson's Aberdeen and Jim McClean's Dundee United rose to the challenge. McClean's United secured their solitary league title in 1983, while Ferguson's Dons were title winners three times in six years. (Unbelievably in all the years since Aberdeen's last triumph, Rangers and Celtic have hoovered up thirty-two consecutive championships!) It was against this background of shifting powers that the 1985–86 Scottish Premier League season started, with the potential champions harder to call than for a generation.

After just one point from their opening three league matches, few punters would have been backing Heart of Midlothian to trouble the trophy engravers, but Hearts were about to hit some very serious form. An unprecedented run of thirty-one league and cup games unbeaten over seven months took the Jam Tarts to the Scottish Cup Final and within touching distance of the title. Led by striker John Robertson's goals and ably supported by John Colquhoun, ex-Rangers duo Sandy Jardine and Sandy Clark and an emerging Craig Levein, Hearts had simply hit the form of their lives.

With one league match left, away at mid-table Dundee, all Hearts needed to do was avoid defeat and Celtic would not be able to catch them for points. Also in Hearts' favour was a goal difference advantage of four – quite rightly now, the punters could hardly get a price on Hearts; they were racing certainties. Goalless at half-time, some Hearts nerves may have been jangling when news came through that Celtic led St Mirren 4-0 at the interval and their goal difference advantage had gone — but still, if the Dens Park game finished goalless the title would belong to Hearts.

The trouble was that Dundee still had a card to play; they brought on striker Albert Kidd, without a goal all season, midway through the second half. With seven minutes left a corner was not cleared in the Hearts penalty area and Kidd lashed it home; just minutes later he was a man transformed as he raced down the right wing before exchanging passes and firing home his second in four minutes to leave Hearts utterly bereft.

As sporting slip-ups go Hearts' 1986 vintage have few peers; to go from assured and deserved triumph to complete meltdown in the space of a few short minutes was almost unheard of. Those with a longer sporting memory, or access to YouTube, might equate Hearts' collapse with the famous 1956 Grand National, in which after a nearly flawless race Devon Loch literally slipped and stumbled within 40 yards of the winning line, allowing ESB to come from a guaranteed second to an unlikely first. Thirty-one years on and counting, Hearts' very own Devon Loch moment has shown few signs of being forgotten; the Scottish duopoly seems as firmly entrenched as ever and the days of the outsider storming home seem very far away.

RED LETTER DAYS

On **1 MARCH 1980** Manchester United were busy chasing Liverpool in the league, pretty much as they had done all decade. United were not a bad side; they were better than most, and Dave Sexton's vintage had added some consistency to their attacking guile of previous seasons. This made what happened at Ipswich's Portman Road all the more surprising, really. United were absolutely thumped by Bobby Robson's men, and ended up on the wrong side of a tennis score line, a thumping 6-0 defeat. And yet it could have been even worse for United. Ipswich were awarded two penalties during the game, one of which had to be retaken, and each kick was saved by United keeper Gary Bailey. The first was a scrambling save to his left from Frans Thijssen; the second saw an outstretched right boot save Kevin Beattie's blast down the middle, and by the time that was retaken Bailey had really got the hang of things and dived smartly to his left again to smother the ball with a superb one-handed block. In a puzzling afternoon, on the ground where his father Roy had made his name as a talented keeper too, Bailey became the first United keeper to save three penalties in a match, and yet he still found time to pick the ball up out of his net on six other occasions! United finished above Ipswich that year, but were two points behind eventual champions Liverpool; they were close, but not yet close enough.

---

26 OCTOBER 1983 became a day to remember for two leading strikers in Division One – both Tony Woodcock and Ian Rush went nap and scored five goals. Rush's sharp-shooting put Luton Town to the sword at Anfield in 6-0 home win while Woodcock's good work came at Villa Park in a 6-2 win for Arsenal. Rush was the more prolific of the two, going on to net forty-seven times that season and was awarded the Golden Boot, as Europe's top scorer. His unerring finishing terrified defenders and goalkeepers throughout the decade. Woodcock did not have the advantage of playing in such a dominant team as Rush – Arsenal spluttered around for much of his time at Highbury – but his credentials were impressive too: a European Cup winner with Forest, an England international and one of the few British players to successfully switch to the Continent with FC Koln.

---

7 NOVEMBER 1984 saw one of the most extraordinary turna-rounds in any European tie when Queens Park Rangers travelled to Belgrade to take on Partizan. Rangers had enjoyed three good years under Terry Venables at the start of the eighties, reaching an FA Cup Final, winning Division Two and then finishing in fifth spot the following year to secure UEFA Cup qualification. Things looked like they were going to get better still after a handsome 6-2 win for Rangers in the first leg, which was played at Highbury as Rangers' plastic pitch was not permitted by UEFA. Now under Alan Mullery's leadership, QPR were not experienced European campaigners and perhaps that shone through. Faced with a hos-tile home crowd, who merrily threw coins and ball bearings at any opponents who moved, Rangers wobbled, collapsed and finally folded to the tune of a 4-0 hammering, enough to put Partizan through on away goals. About 100 QPR fans witnessed the debacle and thirty-three years on it remains their last European venture.

9 APRIL 1988 was the day that 17-year-old Alan Shearer made his full debut for Southampton against Arsenal. Hopes were high on the Saints coaching staff; Shearer was physically strong, he could finish and he had great determination to do well. The thing is, though, that you just never know how young players will fare when they are thrown into the maelstrom of Division One football. Shearer was up against experienced, gnarled old defenders like Sansom and Winterburn, who knew every trick in the book. Yet he was not fazed in the slightest. Ninety minutes and three goals later, Alan Shearer was being applauded off the pitch at The Dell after a five-star debut. With aggression, drive and an expert ability to be in the right place at the right time, he had served notice of just a little of what was to come in the future.

'ACCRINGTON STANLEY? WHO ARE THEY?'

Like any advertising campaign, the Milk Marketing Board needed a line to hang their hat on when they tried to persuade the nation's youth to pick up more of their white stuff in the late eighties. The lines they finally settled on became an unlikely hit in playgrounds up and down the country as two young Liverpool fans were shown wondering where their respective footballing futures would take them. Though not classic Hollywood dialogue, the accents and delivery were faultless:

'Milk? Ugh!'

'It's what Ian Rush drinks.'

'Ian Rush?'

'Yeah. And he says if I don't drink lots of milk, when I grow up I'll only be good enough to play for Accrington Stanley.'

'Accrington Stanley? Who are they?'

'Ex-accly.'

While he might have been considered for a role requiring a very thick Scouse accent himself, Rush's role was strictly limited to off-screen aspirational role-model. Despite being barely old enough to open the fridge successfully, the boys took the word of Rush as the Gospel truth, and if he said drink milk you simply swilled it down. The alternative to guzzling gallons, Rush had decreed, was the path that led only to the footballing wilderness of Accrington, at the time a club who had been out of the Football League for twenty-five years. The killer last lines: "Accrington Stanley? Who are they?" and immediate reply, delivered in slow, guttural, phlegm-infused Scouse accent, "Ex-accly" were mimicked by both lactose-tolerant and intolerant alike, apart from perhaps in Accrington!

MOMENT IN TIME: GORDON SMITH, 1983

In the TV-saturated Premier League era, it has become a bit of a cliché to talk about the days when the FA Cup really did matter – but like many clichés, it contains at least a kernel of truth. In 1983 the FA Cup Final was still held dear by the nation. Fans and neutrals alike tuned in in their millions to see if Brighton's already relegated Seagulls could land a blow for underdogs everywhere by putting one over the more illustrious household names of Manchester United.

Before a ball had even been kicked, the day had started promisingly for Brighton as they became the first finalists to fly into London via helicopter. Jimmy Melia's men then made their next stylish moves on the pitch and took an early lead through Gordon Smith's powerful header. Although United equalised through Frank Stapleton and later led through a superb Ray Wilkins goal, Brighton were not finished. With just three minutes remaining, defender Gary Stevens levelled to take the game into extra time. Inevitably, tired legs on the large, muddy Wembley pitch increased the chances of a slip-up deciding the game and so it was to be, although the mistake was to come from a forward, not a defender; Brighton's number ten, Gordon Smith, was to make headlines for all the wrong reasons.

With seconds remaining of extra time, Albion's Michael Robinson raced past United's Kevin Moran on to a lobbed through ball from Jimmy Case; Robinson impressively turned past a near-statuesque Gordon McQueen in the centre of United's defence and rolled the ball to fellow striker Smith, not 12 yards from goal. With no defender near him and the freedom of the penalty area to enjoy, Smith had only United's prostrate keeper, Gary Bailey, to beat. With 200,000 eyes staring at the imminent winning goal, as the mellifluous tones of

Radio 2's Peter Jones succinctly put it, 'Smith must score.' Somehow, even though it seemed almost harder to miss than to score, Smith fired straight at Bailey's legs and there was no winning goal.

For Bailey, the save represented redemption – four years earlier he had aimlessly waved at a last-minute cross famously turned in by Arsenal's Alan Sunderland to win the cup for the Gunners. For Brighton and for Smith, though, the miss was catastrophic; a 4-0 drubbing in the replay ensured Smith's glorious entry into the headlines and the history books, apparently so assured, was to be erased as his name went straight to the top of the cruellest of 'if onlys' list.

GOLDEN BOOTS

When Gary Lineker went to the Mexico World Cup in 1986, his stock was already high. After transferring from his home-town club, Leicester City, just one season at Everton had brought him a whopping forty goals. And yet the Blues narrowly missed out on a league and cup double, finishing runners-up in both. Lineker had proven beyond all doubt that he could perform at the top level domestically. The question now was could he transfer that to the biggest stage of all?

England started the '86 World Cup poorly, losing to Portugal and only drawing with Morocco. Along the way they also lost two captains – firstly, Bryan Robson to injury and then Ray Wilkins to a red card for throwing the ball at the referee. By the time Lineker lined up to play Poland in the final group match it was win or bust for England; nothing else would see them progress and the portents were not good.

By half-time England led 3-0 courtesy of a Lineker hat-trick, and the game was all but won. Each of the goals were typical of Lineker's predatory penalty box style; two first-time finishes from the edge of the 6-yard box were added to with a nice piece of anticipation, taking advantage of a goalkeeping spill. In Monterrey that day Lineker demonstrated his happy knack of being in the right place at the right time to finish things off, and it was a trait which was to establish him as a stiker of real international quality.

The second round win over Paraguay was another comfortable 3-0 affair and this time Lineker's goals came from even closer to the goal, a 2-yard tap-in and a 6-yard side-foot home. Lineker made scoring look like the easiest job on the field – but he could only do that because of his expert anticipation of the play. He just got to where the ball would come to before everyone else! The controversial quarter-final defeat to Argentina saw Lineker bag yet another close-range effort, this time smartly heading a John Barnes cross downwards into the net, and this left England's number ten as the competition's leading scorer. No one was able to overtake the six-goal haul in the last games and the golden boot was his.

Lineker was never the type of striker who could go and create too many chances for team-mates or who could pick the ball up 30 yards out, hurdle a few challenges and then thump the ball home. If he ever did those things it was occasionally. What was typical Lineker was his expert sense of knowing where to be, his ability to get there quicker than anyone else and his unerring ability to finish; everything a striker needed was everything Lineker had.

TAYLOR

If you could have searched Google in the 1980s and typed in the name Graham Taylor, invariably there would be certain words that always followed – pragmatic, inspirational, even visionary would most likely have popped up. Throughout the 1980s we had no Google, but we did have Graham Taylor giving pretty much a masterclass in club management.

The decade started with Taylor firmly established at Watford's Vicarage Road, having already led the club to two successive promotions, as Division Four champions in 1978 and Division Three runners-up in 1979. Within three years they were at it again, going up for the first time in their history as Second Division runners-up. Questions were asked as to how the Hornets might fare in their first ever season in the top flight, but the answer was simple: very well indeed. They finished second behind Liverpool and provided the league's top scorer in twenty-seven-goal Luther Blissett. The Watford story rolled on to an FA Cup Final appearance twelve months later and Taylor's stock could not have been higher.

After a decade at Watford, Taylor freshened things up by moving to Aston Villa, but the magic touch had not deserted him – instant promotion from the Second Division and a league title challenge at the end of the decade ensured he was the man most talked about to succeed England's departing Bobby Robson. That move was one of the few that did not go Taylor's way, but by then he had more than a decade of excellent club management behind him. So how did he do it?

To take any side from Fourth Division to First Division runners-up within six years was a remarkable achievement and was testament to Taylor's qualities. He had an eye for a player – picking up John Barnes from non-league football for instance. He had fantastic organisation, sometimes practising over fifty corners in a training session, and he had leadership qualities that extended to players, club and even the local community. In a then radical move, he insisted players lived no further than 30 miles from Vicarage Road, and visits to local workplaces and schools and hospitals were included in players' contracts; Taylor simply had a vision of a football club and the energy and nous to make it happen.

You sometimes hear of managers losing the dressing room, or of players not playing for a manager they don't like or respect. Taylor had no such issues, inspiring players to travel with him on his almighty adventure. Several players went up the leagues with Taylor – keeper Steve Sherwood, strikers Ross Jenkins and Luther Blissett – all went from Division Four to One. The many who joined along the way were attracted to a club and a man who were going places.

About the only criticism that was regularly voiced against Taylor was the style of his teams – that they were too direct and that they did not play enough football. In some ways it's a charge that can be made of any team that does not slavishly follow the Arsene Wenger possession-based model; Taylor's teams did not play that sophisticated game. They were more pragmatic. However, they were also very attack-minded and scored a lot of goals. Seventy-four in their first ever season in Division One suggested their forward four, Callaghan, Barnes, Jenkins and Blissett, knew where the goal was.

Taylor wanted the ball forward quickly and for his teams to press high up the pitch, a kind of first-line-of-defence-is-attack theory which, when played properly, can strangle opposition teams. Watford often achieved the desired effect, but mostly through their willingness to quickly get forward and quickly get shooting – in the entertainment business, maybe Taylor's way was not such a bad thing after all.

PLASTIC FANTASTIC

For clubs looking to raise some extra income there was real appeal in the idea of installing all-weather plastic pitches. The pitches would be innovative, a kind of fast-forward leap into football's future, it would be possible to hire them out for community use and they might even help teams adopt a quick-fire passing game. Of the different motives though, probably it was the idea that artificial surfaces could draw in extra revenue that most held sway in the boardrooms of QPR, Oldham, Luton and Preston.

Once Football League agreement was secured, the experiment began at QPR's Loftus Road in 1981. Fans and players alike were eager to see how the surfaces would stand up to the rigours of competitive professional football. Initial reports were mixed as the differences in surface brought clear differences to the games. While the plastic rewarded players and teams who were able to keep the ball moving along the deck at speed, this was not everyone's preferred style. Sides who enjoyed a more combative approach, which was still a key part of football, found themselves at a disadvantage. The full-blooded sliding tackle prohibited itself as the risk of badly burning yourself, unless you happened to have legs made of asbestos, quickly became a disincentive. Goalies routinely resorted to wearing long tracksuit bottoms to prevent carpet burns and players, particularly away ones who were unused to the surface, mistrusted the bounce of the ball. In the early days, spectators wondered about the amount of bounce that hitherto standard footballs were now generating – less of the Adidas tango, more of the ping pong, it sometimes seemed. Oldham manager Joe Royle, a chief beneficiary of the artificial surfaces himself, claimed to have seen a goalkeeper's punt upfield at QPR bounce once only before it went over the opposing crossbar – exaggeration or not, Royle was on to something. The pitches were different to what everyone else played on week in, week out up and down the country. This very simply meant those playing on the pitches the most had an advantage of sorts because of their familiarity.

QPR abandoned their experiment after seven years, and by 1995 artificial surfaces were banned from professional matches. Though today's 3G pitches are much better, there has not been a clamour to start re-laying the plastic; top-division clubs don't need the money and the surface's earlier rejection still lingers. The pitches could still be a godsend for struggling lower league clubs, but for now the football authorities want to maintain some semblance of a level playing field, in the pitches at least. Unlike some of the over-hit passes that zipped along the old artificial surfaces, the vision of future pitches was not misplaced, but for now it might just be filed in the 'sometime in the future' box.

THE THINGS THEY SAY

Tigana. Tigana again. Tigana. Platini. Goooaaalllll

John Motson, BBC

European Championship semi-final, June 1984
France 3 Portugal 2
With six minutes left of extra time in their thrilling Euro '84 semi-final, hosts France trailed Portugal 2-1 and the team orchestrated by Platini, Giresse and Tigana looked to be down and out. The Marseilles crowd though were to experience the ultimate high of snatching victory from probable defeat as first Jean-François Domergue and then Michael Platini turned the game upside down with two late goals. Platini's winning strike, his eighth of the competition, was almost too much for John Motson, whose drawn-out, guttural shriek lived in the memory almost as long as France's sublime football.

HOWARD'S WAY

There are times and moments which can only be regarded as pivotal, as game-changers if you like, when a course or a direction has been altered for good. These kind of moments stay with you, like when you hear Champions League losers will in future qualify for the Europa League, or that Divisions Three and Four will be rebranded as Leagues One and Two, sometimes moments come along which seem to make no sense at the time, but leave an imprint.

Rewind to early 1984 for a League Cup quarter-final at Oxford United's old Manor Ground. Visitors Everton are trailing to Third Division United when Oxford midfielder Kevin Brock inexplicably plays a shocking backpass to his keeper that is so short that it allows Adrian Heath to nip in round the keeper and almost pull up a settee and turn on the TV before slotting home an unlikley equaliser. That one goal is fondly remembered by all Evertonians as it was a massive turning point. Prior to Heath's goal the Goodison Park skies were grey; Howard Kendall's struggling team had not been able to raise even a gallop that season and a cup defeat to lower league opposition might just have put Kendall out of a job. Instead, Everton went on to win the replay, reach the League Cup Final, which was narrowly lost to Liverpool, before getting back on the saddle in the FA Cup, returning to Wembley and this time coming home with the cup after beating Watford 2-0.

The 1984 FA Cup final established Everton as a team on the up and despite starting (and ending funnily enough) the new league season with two successive defeats the points were soon stacking up. The team really set down a marker during a purple patch in autumn; one week reigning champions Liverpool were beaten at Anfield by Graeme Sharp's net-burster, and then the following week Manchester United were simply taken to pieces at Goodison in a 5-0 thrashing. Ten wins out of thirteen seemed to signal Evertons' intent – they were ready to challenge again

In goal, the peerless Southall was a towering presence for any oppositon strikers to get past and he was ably protected by the speedy Ratcliffe and redoubtable Mountfield in front of him. Further forward Bracewell and Reid snapped and snarled, destroying opposing attacks before starting their own, while wide men Steven and Sheedy added guile and goals to the mix. Formerly a Liverpool reserve, Sheedy had a wand of a left foot, regularly arcing free kicks into top corners and offering the sort of precise delivery the Royal Mail could only

dream of. At the top of the team were more gems. Though
often not first choice, Adrain Heath had skill, he could finish
and just seemed to annoy defenders. Graeme Sharp led the
line with strength and aggression, scoring some super goals
along the way, most notably his goal of the season screamer at
Anfield in October which seemed to signal Evertons' intent –
they were ready to challenge again. In addition to this potent
mix came Andy Gray, a Scottish forward with courage, touch
and an eye for goal. Gray had once been sold by Aston Villa
for almost one and a half million to Wolves, but injuries had
seemed to take their toll and by the time Howard Kendall paid
a much reduced £250,000 in November 1983, people were
not sure the outlay would be justified. Gray soon proved any
doubts were misplaced with some electrifying performances
for Everton, perhaps most memorably in the European Cup
Winners Cup semi-final against Bayern Munich in April
1985 when his one goal and two assists steered Everton to
their first European final.

Those who were inside Goodison that night swear the stands
shook as Evertonians bellowed, roared and screamed their boys
on. Trailing 1-0 at half-time, both on the night and on aggregate, the second half comeback had a touch of the Lazarus
about it. With no little skill and some enormous reservoirs of
determination Everton simply battered Bayern into submis-
sion. Weeks later a convincing demolition of Rapid Vienna in
the Cup Winners Cup final gave Everton their first European
trophy. They coupled it with that year's league championship;
the trophy room shelves would soon need extending.

As every Everton fan would tell you, what happened next
became as much a moment of great significance as Kevin
Brock's misplaced backpass eighteen months earlier. The
1985 European Cup final between Liverpool and Juventus
turned into the horrifying Heysel disaster and one of the
consequences of that was that English teams were banned
from European competitions for five years. For the Goodison
Park regulars this was more than an inconvenience; on their

footballing merit alone, Everton had every right to feel they would have been one of the leading contenders for the European Cup of 1986. They had earnt, and were now being denied, the right to compete at Europe's highest level.

Some say Everton's protracted decline can be traced back to that ban after Heysel, although two more FA Cup final appearances in four years and a further league title in 1987 show the team still had plenty to offer. How far Howard Kendall might have been able to take the team on in Europe can only be a matter for speculation now, but it is a matter of fact that he had assembled a highly stylish and successful team, not so unlike the one he had graced in the 1970 league championship year. Like a master alchemist Kendall had taken his various elements and forged them into something special – albeit briefly, Everton had been the best once more.

THE NUMBERS GAME

Some more number-crunching for the statistically-minded to be getting on with ...

£4,250,000 was the figure Marseille paid Tottenham for England winger Chris Waddle in July 1989. By the end of the 1980s this figure was the highest ever fee involving a British player, and considering Waddle's impact in France – three league titles and a European Cup Final appearance – the huge investment paid dividends.

85 was the number of home games Liverpool went unbeaten for in all competitions, from January 1978 to January 1981. The run incorporated league, FA Cup, League Cup, European Cup and Super Cup fixtures and saw Liverpool win a mightily impressive sixty-nine of the eighty-five fixtures, reflecting their pre-eminence of the time. When soon to be relegated Leicester City turned up it seemed to be business as usual as Liverpool led by a goal at the interval. Very improbably, the Foxes levelled before Jim Melrose's winner brought the curtain down on a time of unparalleled Liverpool invincibility.

6 years of English dominance in the European Cup finally ended in 1983, when Germany's Hamburg pipped Juventus 1-0 in that year's final. Three different English teams had shared the previous six successive triumphs: Liverpool in 1977, 1978 and 1981, followed by Nottingham Forest in 1979 and 1980 before Aston Villa in 1982. Villa and Liverpool were not a million miles away in '83 either, both losing quarter-finals, but despite Liverpool's 1984 victory over Roma, an era of total English dominance was coming to a close.

0 was the number of points a highly fancied England squad accrued at Euro '88. After finishing strongly at the Mexico World Cup in 1986 and boasting some impressive talent in Robson, Hoddle, Lineker and Footballer of the Year John Barnes, hopes were justifiably high. However, just about everything that could go wrong did: three tough opponents, two narrow defeats, to Ireland and Holland, and one out-of-sorts striker in Gary Lineker who would soon be diagnosed with hepatitis. Robson's men achieved little, but within two years they almost conquered the world!

ESCAPE FROM REALITY

The trouble with films about football, or probably most sports, is that when you come to the really exciting dramatic parts on which a whole two hours' viewing might hinge, it can quite easily all go pear-shaped. If you have an actor who can't kick a ball straight, or, alternatively, a footballer who cannot mumble two words together, then whole plot lines disintegrate and the appearance of reality is shattered. It was with this in mind that the producers of *Escape to Victory* hit upon what seemed like the perfect recipe: grab some well-known actors, with a bit of form behind them, like a Michael Caine, or a Sylvester Stallone say, and blend them with some real-life footballers, similarly well regarded, perhaps a World Cup winner like Pelé, or Osvaldo Ardiles, add a dash of mid-field enforcer John Wark and flesh out the mix with a hint of defensive kingpin in Ipswich's Russell Osman – who could resist a bite of the action? While the idea sounded plausible on paper, we all know you don't make great films on paper; it's what happens out on the celluloid that counts ...

The film's plot revolves around some Allied prisoners of war who are in a German prison camp who have to play an exhibition game against a German team. The match gives a perfect opportunity for the prisoners to escape their confines, via the sewer system, which can be handily accessed via the players' showers. At half-time with the Germans leading 4-1 the French resistance arrive in the dressing room to rescue the players, only for the boys to decide to play on and ditch the escape plan until the game is finished. The surprising decision to risk further imprisonment at the hands of the Nazis in order to gain a credible draw or even win stretches credibility for sure, but we should remember the film was never billed as a Graham Taylor style fly-on-the-wall documentary – just a bit of fun.

Encouraged by Osman's exhortations, Michael Caine picks up the refrain 'Yes, we can win this' and his Obama-style line soon works on Stallone, within moments the Rocky star is hitching up his shorts waiting for the second half to commence. Ardiles soon dribbles through almost the entire German team to reduce the deficit and by the time the injured Pelé rejoins the fray there is only one goal in it. In a fashion that not even the script-writers could predict, Pelé is soon bicycle-kicking the Allies to 4-4 with a majestic overhead kick, it's worth remembering that these were the days before CGI, so Brazil's finest would have had to actually do that himself – anecdotes suggest he needed only one take before belting the ball home. Before the prisoners inevitably escape, mixing with the crowd rather than travelling down the sewer, Stallone has time to magnificently save a last minute penalty and an honourable draw is achieved. Some critics lambasted the film, pointing to implausible plots and some acting that was as wooden as the stands, but perhaps that misses the point; for a bit of harmless fun, with a famous face or two, it's simply *Boys' Own* stuff.

FINE MARGINS

Stirling Albion 20 Selkirk 0
Scottish Cup Round 1, December 1984
Some ninety-nine years after the highest verifiable result in a professional football match anywhere, when Arbroath famously walloped Bon Accord 36-0, statisticians were racing for the record books again after an extraordinary afternoon at Stirling Albion's Annfield Stadium.

At the time of the Scottish Cup fixture Albion were hovering unremarkably around in the lower half of the Scottish Second Division while Selkirk were a modest Scottish Border Amateur League club. There were no previous portents of

Stirling hitting teams for double figures, or Selkirk shipping a score – which made what took place at Annfield that afternoon even more astonishing.

Although Albion led by five at the interval, it turned out to be just the warm-up act, as they hit fifteen more in the second period. Selkirk's rookie keeper, Richard Taylor, admitted he had only been in nets for a year prior to the game, but such was the size of the pasting Stirling administered that Selkirk might have fielded three keepers and still been roundly beaten. Happily, the drubbing did not dent Selkirk spirits for too long; when making their two permitted substitutions, in the days before electronic blinking boards, the Selkirk coaching staff displayed a fine sense of gallows humour as they held up each single board from one to eleven!

The match did make it into the record books as the highest recorded winning margin in British football in the whole of the twentieth century. What lasting damage or impetus the mauling was responsible for is less clear to ascertain. Selkirk recovered from their mauling to win the Border Amateur League B Division, while the impetus it gave Stirling in the rest of their cup run is open to debate – Albion slipped to a 2-1 defeat to Cowdenbeath in Round Two!

Liverpool 10 Oulun Palloseura 1
European Cup Round 1, October 1980

In the days of the European Cup things were quite straightforward, really. Prior to the redrawing of the maps of Eastern Europe and the USSR there were fewer teams in the competition, only bona fide champions were allowed to compete, and there were still several nations who had not quite got the hang of professional football as a competitive business. At the turn of the eighties the script was simple: you played a couple of games against very weak opponents, racked up a hatful of goals in the home leg and looked forward to a decent match in the last sixteen or the last eight. In 1980, Liverpool had learnt their lines and gave a textbook performance on how to demolish weaker opponents. After a 1-1 draw in Finland, in the return tie at Anfield Liverpool simply played football of a level the Finns could not get close to.

Graeme Souness and Terry McDermott each grabbed hat-tricks as the mismatch played out, though Oulu could claim to have benefited from the learning experience as they made a losing return to Anfield just twelve months later, this time going down by only 7-0. While the *Liverpool Echo* summed things up neatly with their final line of their match report, commenting that 'it was all so terribly easy', perhaps the best line of the night went to the Radio Two commentator who, after goal seven or eight simply declared 'that is the finish of the Finnish!'

Liverpool 10 Fulham 0
League Cup Round 2, September 1986

When Fulham came calling for a League Cup tie at Anfield in September 1986 the days of squad rotation and blooding your promising young players in a cup competition had not even been dreamt of. To play anything other than your full complement of first-teamers was anathema to leading clubs and so it was that Fulham of the Third Division lined up against Liverpool's full artillery.

A glance at the Liverpool team sheet revealed the usual stellar names, Rush and Dalglish, Whelan and Wark, Hansen and Lawrenson; it was clear Liverpool meant business. The Reds were four goals to the good at half-time and added another half-dozen in the second period, giving one of the league's younger managers, and future England number two, Ray Lewington plenty to ponder before the return leg. Faced with the unlikely prospect of overturning a ten-goal deficit, Fulham rallied a little at Craven Cottage for the home leg and second time around only lost 3-2, but as a contest the tie was almost over before it started.

West Ham United 10–0 Bury
League Cup Round 2, October 1983

Nineteen-year-old Tony Cottee made most of the headlines in this record-breaking win for West Ham, by grabbing four of the ten goals that West Ham put past Bury. In eighty-eight years the Hammers had never before hit double figures in any senior match and the goal glut came after only a slender 2-1 win at Gigg Lane in the first leg.

The second leg was a different story as Bury were blown away, shipping five goals in each half. Had the visitors converted the penalty they were awarded when trailing just 1-0 on the night the scoreboard workers may not have been quite so busy. Despite Bury's defence being pulled to pieces all night long, Hammers boss John Lyall nonetheless spotted something he liked in the opposition back four and signed Bury centre half Paul Hilton just a few months later!

Manchester City 10-1 Huddersfield
Division Two, November 1987

In November 1987, City were struggling to enjoy life in Division Two; for every win there seemed to be a defeat and a draw, and the prospects of bouncing straight back after the previous year's relegation were not promising. They were, however, in better shape than opponents Huddersfield Town, who arrived at Maine Road bottom of the table and now under the inexperienced leadership of the recently arrived ex-striking hero Malcolm McDonald.

As is so often the case with extraordinary matches, there were few portents that anything strange was on the way at all; the air in Manchester had not been declared to be raining goals, and none of the team's strikers had been reported as being 'on fire' any time lately. At kick-off, nearly 20,000 fans had no reason to suspect anything out of the ordinary was about to unfold, but ninety minutes later the fans had just witnessed a once-in-a-century-match in which someone probably should have called the RSPCA for Huddersfield's Terriers.

All afternoon almost everything that City hit flew into the Town net – ten goals from twelve goal attempts. Town had even more attempts on goal, yet scored only once, a penalty to make it 9-1! Players and managers agreed that Huddersfield had started well and even looked the more likely side for twenty minutes or so. Until Paul Stewart made it 2-0 just before the half hour, Town were certainly in the contest.

Four ahead at half-time, City continued to tear into their opponents in the second period, adding five more before Town converted a late penalty. With seconds remaining, David White raced through a now non-existent Town defence to round the keeper and secure double figures. The goal-fest did leave one tricky issue to be resolved though – how could you pick a Man of the Match when three players, Stewart, Adcock and White, had each scored hat-tricks? One bright spark in the City boardroom had the answer and gave the award to the non-scoring midfielder Paul Simpson! *

Gillingham 10 Chesterfield 0
Division Three, September 1987

The Medway Towns are rightly known for many things. As a child Charles Dickens lived in Chatham and his work often references the local area; just a mile or two up the road is the magnificent Rochester Cathedral, the second oldest in the country; and almost next door to that is the fantastically pre-served twelfth-century Keep of Rochester Castle. The place is jam-packed with historical and literary significance. However, for a week or two back in 1987, Charles Dickens and his history-loving pals had to take a back seat as Gillingham Football Club made some pretty impressive history of their own – scoring no less than a whopping eighteen league goals in successive home matches.

---

* One nice footnote to the Maine Road massacre was that the author's brother-in-law hobbled along to the game after being injured in a Saturday morning match in which his own team had just been beaten 10-1!

First up were Southend United on a late August afternoon at sleepy Priestfield, and it was The Shrimpers who were left feeling as if they had been boiled alive as they shipped eight goals to Keith Peacock's men, including four from striker Steve Lovell. Prior to that afternoon The Gills had not registered a goal in their opening two league matches, but something was clearly in the Medway waters. The Southend game became merely the hors d'oeuvre before the main dish the following week – a ten-goal feast against Chesterfield.

After such a bountiful start to the season, hopes were understandably high that Gillingham would go on to enjoy a promotion-challenging year. But these early portents were misleading. They found themselves on the wrong end of a 6-0 scoreline at Aldershot in the New Year which led to manager Peacok's sacking, and the season tailed off from there, finishing with a run of just two league wins in twelve, The Gills finished a very mediocre thirteenth. Although three decades on the double-figure thrashing remains the highest score ever recorded in a Third Division game, for Gills fans it was one just more false dawn

MOMENT IN TIME: DIEGO MARADONA, 1986

In the unrelenting heat of the Azteca Stadium, Mexico City, in front of over 114,000 fans, England lined up against Argentina for their 1986 World Cup quarter-final with momentum and confidence high. A poor start had been forgotten after convincing victories against Poland and Paraguay which saw Beardsley create and Lineker finish chances. It seemed England had a chance against an Argentina team, who, if you took star turn Maradona out of the equation, were far from extraordinary.

The first half was energy-sapping as Argentina kept the ball better, but there were no goals – Robson's men were unquestionably still in the contest. Shortly after the interval everything changed within a few minutes which displayed both football, and Maradona himself, at their very best and very worst.

As England struggled to repel another Argentinian attack, Steve Hodge arced a clearance back towards the oncoming Shilton. England's number one was a tall, bulky man, renowned for his decision-making, speed of thought and athleticism; in half a second he was out to and ready to collect a high ball for the thousandth time in an impeccable career. That Shilton could be outjumped by the 5ft 5in Maradona seemed unlikely, if not impossible; it defied logic, and it turned out, the laws of the game. Maradona challenged Shilton for the dropping ball as was his right to do, but the fact he reached it a fraction before the goalkeeper was because his outstretched arm made up the gap in height; his hand, not his head, had craftily nudged the ball into the empty net. Immediately Shilton and half the team protested vehemently, but the referee's whistle signalled goal and England faced the twin blows of going behind and to a goal that should never have stood.

As the watching millions spluttered outrage and maybe even expletives at their televisions, just moments later Maradona went from villain to victor as he scored one of the most memorable goals of that or any World Cup. Collecting the ball inside his own half, Maradona pirouetted past Peter Reid before galloping towards, and then straight through, the England defence; Butcher and Fenwick floundered, the advancing Shilton stumbled as Argentina's number ten rounded almost half the team before rolling the ball into an empty net. It was a moment as sublime as his earlier goal had been fraudulent – simply peerless play from a master.

In England there was no debate. Perhaps or perhaps not aided by the febrile post-Falklands atmosphere, public opinion was unequivocal. Maradona had cheated, he was a disgrace and it was better to lose with honour than to win tainted with disgrace. Outside of these shores though, some gave Maradona's antics a begrudging nod, it was merely another way to seek an advantage, like simulation nowadays, and if it went your way, so be it.

An unrepentant Maradona poured salt on the wound by cheekily christening his goal the 'Hand of God', though the hand of a cheat was a more prosaic alternative. Days later, in the semi-final, he slalomed past the Belgian defence in almost identical fashion as if to confirm his stature as the world's greatest individual talent. Yet when he lifted the World Cup trophy at the end of the tournament, for many millions around the world Maradona, and the game itself, were more than a little tainted by the number ten's antics.

THE FINAL HURDLE

When England played South Africa at cricket in the final test of 1939, it was agreed in advance to just keep on playing and playing until a result was achieved, regardless of time. It was a bit like that when Arsenal met Liverpool in the 1980 FA Cup semi-final, they just kept on playing each other too – four cup semi-finals in nineteen days (a second drawn league match of the season was sandwiched in between to make it five meetings in less than three weeks), until a result could finally be eked out in what very nearly became football's own timeless test.

At the time of the first meeting, both sides were enjoying strong seasons; Liverpool were front-runners in the league and had a league and cup double in their sights, while Arsenal were a little off the pace in the league but were looking for cup success in the form of a third successive FA Cup final appearance and an already secured first European final in the Cup Winners' Cup too.

The first meeting between the sides at Hillsborough did not produce a goal, and the next two replays, both at Villa Park, brought two 1-1 draws after last-gasp rescue acts. Even though it had a smaller capacity than Villa Park, Coventry's Highfield Road stadium was chosen for the third replay, and almost 40,000 raised the roof (at least on the three sides of the ground which had a roof) in anticipation of another titanic struggle. For the only time in the six meetings between the teams that year, there finally was a winner as Arsenal's Brian Talbot flung himself goalwards to head home the game's only goal.

While Liverpool went on to retain their league title, for Arsenal the two huge finals represented two huge disappointments. At Wembley against second division West Ham United, the Gunners simply ran out of ammunition and could not break down West Ham's sturdy defence. An early Trevor

Brooking goal, famously headed by the man who only ever used his head in the cerebral sense, was enough to take the cup back to Upton Park.

Just four days later Arsenal had to pick themselves up for the Cup Winners Cup final against Mario Kempes' Valencia for game number sixty-eight of a monumental seventy-game season; the gruelling schedule undoubtedly had an effect on the team, as this was a time still way before the days of squad rotation and players just had to go and get on with whatever demands were thrown at them. Brian Talbot famously started all seventy games and was only subbed twice!

By the time of kick-off in Brussels, the struggles and battles of earlier rounds were catching up with the team both physically and mentally; Arsenal had simply run out of gas and were unable to repeat some of the incisive attacking football of earlier months. The game drifted towards a penalty shootout in which Graham Rix fluffed his lines and the cup went to Spain; for the second time in four days Arsenal had fallen at the final hurdle. The Gunners had won many battles that year, but could not quite claim the war.

WHITESIDE

Schoolboys used to have to read *Roy of the Rovers* comics to hear about sensational feats and unbelievable goals from kids still young enough to pay half-fare on the school bus. That was before Norman Whiteside emerged, as a strapping 16-year-old, into Manchester United's first team in May 1982. Whiteside would soon be putting the comic-strip creators out of work, as whatever storylines they could dream up, the Belfast boy wonder would top them all with an instantly stellar career.

When Whiteside debuted against Brighton at the Goldstone Ground in April 1982 he became United's youngest player since Duncan Edwards. His first senior goal followed weeks later and before he could even book a summer holiday he was snapped up by Northern Ireland's World Cup squad. Impressive performances in Northern Ireland's run were bolstered by the fact that Whiteside had taken Pelé's revered record of youngest player to appear in the World Cup finals. Before even ten senior games, Whiteside had left an indelible mark on football history, but he was only getting started.

Strong beyond his years, with an immaculate touch and an eye for goal, Whiteside had everything required for an outstanding career in the higher echelons of the game. In his first full season he twice set records for being a youngest ever cup final scorer – in a 2-1 League Cup Final defeat to Liverpool and in a 4-0 replay win over Brighton to win the FA Cup.

Whiteside's goal against Liverpool was forward play at its finest as he perfectly controlled a long ball on his chest with back to gaol and three defenders in close attendance. The sharpest of turns left one of Britain's best ever centre backs, Alan Hansen, for dead. In an instant, before the covering defenders could get near to him, like a gun-slinging cowboy in a duel, Whiteside, took aim and fired, straight and true into the bottom of the net. Still only 17, there seemed to be nothing the young man could not do.

Two years later, a Wembley winner against Everton, again showcased Whiteside's vision. To even think of shooting from the left-hand corner of the penalty area with defenders in close attendance seemed audacious; to pull it off was spectacular. Arguably that goal represented Whiteside's peak, as both he and United lost their way over the following seasons – their talented squad never completed a title challenge.

As injuries became more prominent, Whiteside seemed to stall at United and a later move to high-flying Everton, at still only 24, saw one decent season. It proved to be a respite rather than a recovery however, as continuing knee troubles finally defeated Whiteside and his career ended prematurely at the age of just 26. Like the brightest of shooting stars he had blazed an extraordinary trail, but, sadly, he was destined not to last.

DARKEST DAYS: 1985

By the time the 1980s dawned, British football had become increasingly synonymous with spiralling hooliganism. Instances of spectator disorder, both inside and close to football stadiums, had started to make as many headlines as the action on the pitch; sometimes overcrowded stadiums, often meagrely resourced and unsupervised, did little to challenge a culture that tolerated a passive acceptance of poor conditions and poor behaviour – going to the match could have risks attached.

It was in this bleak climate that English football was to experience some of its lowest points. In March 1985, the then rare treat of a live televised cup tie between Luton and Millwall soured the nation's screens as pitched battles broke out across the pitch in full view of watching millions. Sadly, lessons were not learnt quickly and before some knee-jerk government initiatives of ID card schemes and alcohol bans could be set in place, various club chairmen started to attract publicity for increasingly stringent responses. Ken Bates at Chelsea wanted fans behind electric fences, while David Evans at Luton succeeded for a time in securing a complete ban on away fans.

Just two months later, on 11 May, football's two biggest scourges, poor conditions and poor behaviour, coincided terribly and tragically. Birmingham City and Leeds United fans fought running battles at City's St Andrew's ground that resulted in 145 injured police officers and 125 arrests as crowd disorder plumbed new depths. Amid the scenes of riot and mayhem a wall collapsed and, heartbreakingly, a 15-year-old was caught under the falling rubble. He later died from the injuries he sustained.

On the very same afternoon, a little over 120 miles north, the planned promotion party of Third Division champions Bradford City was to turn into, at the time, the worst sporting disaster in England. An antiquated wooden stand caught alight, probably from a discarded cigarette, and within minutes fifty-six spectators had lost their lives. The decades-long neglect of spectator facilities meant Bradford was far from the only club to offer outdated and dangerous stadiums for their fans. What happened at Valley Parade, could have happened at many, many clubs where crummy and crumbling terraces and stands were the norm, not the exception. The tacit acceptance of both the lamentable facilities and lamentable fans behaviour had now almost reached a tipping point, but it would take further tragedies to force the footballing authorities to take decisive actions.

Eighteen days after the disasters at Birmingham and Bradford, what was then known as the 'English disease' was exported to the Heysel stadium in Brussels for the European Cup final between Liverpool and Juventus. As fans across Europe settled down on their sofas and armchairs to watch the two highly regarded teams slug it out for the continent's most prestigious title, catastrophe struck. Prior to kick-off spectators taunted each other, almost in routine fashion, before some Liverpool supporters charged towards their Italian rivals. Ineffective segregation and poor policing played a part as panic broke out among terrified Juventus fans, who simply tried to run to safety. Within moments a crush and a collapsed wall and had led to fatalities — thirty-eight on the night, later to become thirty-nine. Bans from European competition and withdrawn domestic television deals soon followed as it seemed that the perfect storm of mismanagement of stadiums and misbehaviour of fans had led English football to its lowest point.

THE ARM OF THE LAW

The trouble with cup finals is that they can often be more anticipated than they are remembered, and after nearly eighty minutes of the 1985 FA Cup Final between champions Everton and high-flying Manchester United, the contest could only have been characterised as dull. If ever a match needed some drama, it was this one; thankfully with just over ten minutes left the unlikely triumvirate of Everton schemer Peter Reid, United stopper Kevin Moran and refereeing police officer Peter Willis combined to give the watching millions the ultimate talking point.

When Everton's Peter Reid intercepted a rare loose touch from Paul McGrath, United's Kevin Moran seemed well positioned to cover. However, Moran was just a fraction of a second late in his covering tackle and Reid was sent tumbling across the turf. As Moran had been United's last man in defence, officer Willis, like a judge in a courtroom, had a decision to make. Although Reid was far from United's net, referee Willis deemed the foul to have prevented a clear goal-scoring opportunity, and he opted to send Moran off.

After almost sixty years of Wembley cup finals Moran became the first player to be sent off in the showpiece occasion. The following days saw continuing media debates as to whether the decision was justified, though interestingly enough the ITV pundits Mick Channon, Jimmy Greaves and Ian St John, all suitably straight-talking and forthright, were united and vehement in their condemnation of Willis: 'an imposter calling himself a referee,' Channon harshly trilled.

Thanks to Norman Whiteside's stunning extra-time winner, it was the United team who climbed Wembley's fabled thirty-nine steps to collect the cup. In typical cup-winning fashion all the players went up, bedecked in hats and scarves and sporting the broadest of grins – all the players, that is, apart from Kevin

Moran. The disgraced defender was not allowed to collect his
own medal for several days while the FA decided if he should
be allowed to or not. There was no such prevarication from
Peter Willis though, who later declared with certainty that he
had simply 'applied the laws of the game'.

HOUDINI AT HIGHFIELD ROAD

The Coventry City team of the early to mid 1980s are not
on anyone's list of stylish outfits of the decade; the Sky Blues
were perennially entrenched in relegation dogfights and for
three years in a row the battles went down to last-day decid-
ers. Yet even when probable odds, good sense and simple
rules of football logic were applied, somehow the Sky Blues
remained afloat.

The 1984 escape set the template; decent pre-Christmas
form (including a 4-0 humbling of soon-to-be-European
champions Liverpool) was followed by a precipitous collapse
in the New Year and after shipping eight goals at Southampton
in April, the team looked certainties for the drop. However,
ex-City striker Mick Ferguson, back on loan from relegation
rivals Birmingham City, began to make his presence felt; three
goals in the final half-dozen games enabled City to scramble
over the finishing line. In the final match City led Norwich
2-1 with just a minute left when Norwich striker Robert
Rosario rose to powerfully steer the ball well beyond City
keeper Suckling. As almost 14,000 fans held their breath, the
ball bounced back off the upright – the margin could not
have been tighter.

After much talk along the lines of 'never again' City found
themselves even further up the creek without a proverbial
paddle just twelve months later. A flu virus within the club
had led to postponements and meant most teams finished
their fixtures ahead of the Sky Blues. With three games left

to play, nothing less than nine points was needed to go above already-finished Norwich. The first game brought a narrow 1-0 win at relegated Stoke, who hit the bar with a late penalty; the second game brought another 1-0 victory, this time secured via Brian Kilcline's net-burster with only six minutes remaining. The unlikeliest of escapes was completed on a dazzling, sunny, Sunday morning when champions Everton were the visitors. City saved their best performance for the final match of the year as they tore into an admittedly jaded Everton and came out on top 4-1. For the first time all season City won three games in a row, and their timing could not have been better.

The final part of the triumvirate of escapes came in 1986, when once again the promises of progress had failed to materialise. After a customary drubbing at Anfield, manager Don Mackay resigned with the team one place above the relegation zone and just three games left. Without a permanent successor in mind the club appointed almost the only people they could at such short notice – two ex-players who were still on the backroom staff, George Curtis and John Sillett. The two wise old heads did the trick as City took six points from nine to stage another Lazarus-like recovery.

All the escapology and last-minute heroics had hardened the team, though, and when twelve months later they found themselves in an FA Cup Final in the Wembley sunshine the now familiar routine of Coventry having to win their last game of the season was adhered to. The team that went on to beat Tottenham included eight of the side from the previous year's do–or–die last-game scenario; this time it was from Houdinis to heroes in twelve short months.

THE THINGS THEY SAY

It's up for grabs now!

Brian Moore, ITV

Division One, May 1989
Liverpool 0 Arsenal 2
ITV's erudite Brain Moore called it exactly right as Arsenal midfielder Michael Thomas burst through the Liverpool rearguard with seconds left of the title decider in May 1989. Thomas simultaneously silenced Anfield terraces, Liverpool pubs and half the country's living rooms when he prodded home past an aghast Grobbelaar to secure Arsenal's first title in eighteen years with just seconds of the season left. As denouements go, it was pure Hollywood

TV TIMES

Football coverage in the eighties was about as far away from the current media landscape as it is possible to imagine; there were no rolling sports news channels, hardly any live matches and, for a time in late 1985, no televised football whatsoever. Before collective shakes of the head overcome those of us of a certain age, as we ponder a life without instant access to super-slow-mo replays, Robbie Savage's hair and a grinning Richard Keys, it's worth remembering what we did have to satiate our foot-balling appetites – we had *Football Focus* and *Saint and Greavsie*!

For most of the decade, apart from the occasional England game or a midweek edition of Harry Carpenter's *Sportsnight*, the Saturday lunchtime slot was your fill for football punditry. In truth, the football menu was less à la carte and more greasy spoon. Like a trucker in a roadside café, we could only feast on what was available on the menu – and it wasn't much!

The BBC presented *Football Focus*, usually a little after midday, fronted by ex-Arsenal keeper Bob Wilson. Being the BBC, jackets and ties were de rigueur, and despite Wilson's cheeriness a certain formality persisted. That said *Football Focus* was a worthy look at the footballing world, which would sometimes venture outside of the top divisions. Wilson's show was the standard mix of action, studio chat and previews of the weekend's matches; supplemented by large dollops of roving reporters Garth Crooks and Tony Gubba, the show thrived. Football action and football chat were the key ingredients in the show, and the template that it set continues to this day. It is testament to its enduring quality that the programme still runs decades later in a largely recognisable format.

If the BBC had cornered the market in sensible appraisals of the week's action, ITV needed to be different in their own offering – and boy, were they different! *Saint and Greavsie* was conceived as an extension of the fun and games that former strikers of the sixties Ian St John and Jimmy Greaves used to present during *On the Ball*, ITV's own lunchtime football slot. When *World of Sport* finished in 1985, it meant no more *On the Ball*, leaving ITV with a hole in their scheduling which they needed to plug. The idea was for an alternative view of the football world, still based around current football, but with comedy – the perfect vehicle for St John and Greaves, who had been fine-tuning their double act for some time. If it was before your time, think *Soccer Am*, minus the self-promoting current or recent pro and with a resident straight-talking, politically-incorrect uncle in the corner!

The more restrained St John fed the punchlines to Greaves, who delivered gag after gag, and funnily enough, audiences loved it. Though both presenters undoubtedly knew their stuff, they never set out to be highbrow, instead making a direct pitch for the belly-laughing fans on the settee before they left for the match. For seven years, until the advent of Sky in 1992, the show worked well. In a time-honoured combination St John was the straight man, to Greaves' comic turn, a kind of Syd Little to Eddie Large combination!

Of course, by the end of the eighties, times were beginning to change. The first shoots of satellite tv were sprouting and the days of the BBC / ITV duopoly were soon to end. Yet while they had the nation's undivided attention, the two main broadcasters fed football fans a diet they still largely consume today – serious analysis with just a dash of boyish humour.

HANDS ON THE CUP

The finale of the 1985/86 European Cup brought together two teams both looking for a first triumph in Europe's most prestigious competition: Terry Venables' stylish Barcelona took on the Romanian army team Steaua Bucharest.

Venables' had already endeared himself to the Nou Camp regulars by steering Barca to a league championship in his first full season, and to be pitted against Bucharest, a team of much more modest resources and renown, seemed to be the ideal chance for the Catalans to finally lift their first European crown.

Buoyed by the vast majority of the 70,000 fans in Seville's Estadio Ramón Sánchez Pizjuán, Venables' men were expected to be too strong for their Romanian opponents, yet as the match wore on the Spaniards were unable to turn possession into much goalmouth action and the game meandered into extra time. No goal-scoring heroes emerged in the extra half-hour and so the lottery of penalties was to once again decide the cup.

After two hours of little incident in open play, the cauldron of Seville was about to be lit up by the 6ft 4in moustachioed, curly-haired Romanian goalkeeper, Helmut Ducadam. The first

Barca three penalties were fired low to Ducadam's right, and three times the Bucharest keeper sprang down to keep out each effort. The second save was the pick of them – a stupendous one-handed effort at the right-hand post. Ducadam's transformation from eighties keeper with slightly dubious haircut to footballing superhero was completed within just minutes. After Bucharest edged 2-0 ahead in the shoot-out, Ducadam then etched his name in the goalkeeping pantheon by becoming the first keeper to ever save an astonishing four consecutive penalties in a European final, this time simply diving to his left to make what was by then a pretty routine stop.

For Ducadam, the night in Seville represented the ultimate goalkeeping shoot-out display, one that is unlikely to ever be equalled, never mind bettered. Ducadam's heroics gave Bucharest their first, and so far only, victory in the European Cup. Although they did go on to reach another final three years later, their heroic keeper was destined to play no further part for Steaua. The display of athleticism, agility and nerve was to be Ducadam's final significant act as a footballer, as just weeks later, at the age of only 27, he was cruelly struck down with thrombosis. He never played for Bucharest again, leaving only the very highest of high spots as his signature.

MERSEY UNITED

At one point in the 1980s Everton and Liverpool fans could have been forgiven for booking their Wembley hotels at the start of the season, they were there so often for FA Cup finals, League Cup finals and Charity Shields. As both teams continued their winning ways, it was only a matter of time before the red and blue halves of Merseyside collided at Wembley. In fact, three times in five years the city of Liverpool had to decamp down to Wembley to contest cup finals – one League Cup and two FA Cup finals.

The first meeting was in the spring of 1984 when Howard Kendall's improving men squared up to Joe Fagan's soon-to-be-treble winners. After spending the first half of the season struggling in the lower reaches of the league, Everton's form had improved, but Liverpool were looking for a third consecutive League Championship and an unbelievable fourth consecutive League Cup win. The game was interesting, even absorbing, but not laden with goalmouth action and it finished goalless after extra time. Decades later though, Everton fans still point to what looked like a very clear handball by Alan Hansen to deny Adrian Heath a certain goal; mystifyingly, Hansen wasn't booked, nor did he concede a penalty. That decision mattered a great deal when three days later in a Maine Road replay Graeme Souness scored the only goal to take the League Cup back to Anfield for the fourth year running. Everton had lost, but only narrowly, and the fact they ran that year's European Cup winners so close suggested blue skies ahead at Goodison Park.

Two years later, with both sides having each secured a league title in between, the teams met again, this time for the 1986 FA Cup final. Liverpool stood to become only the third winners of the league and cup domestic double in a century if they made it, while Everton wanted something to show for a season in which they had lost their own league title to the men across Stanley Park.

This time it was Everton who started the stronger; Lineker's greyhound-speed took him past Alan Hansen on to Peter Reid's through-ball, and when Grobbelaar saved his first effort Lineker was there to put the rebound home and give Everton a deserved lead. For the first ten minutes of the second half it was Everton still on top. Some uncharacteristic nervy defending from Liverpool culminated in keeper Grobbelaar exploding in rage at full–back Jim Beglin. The Reds were clearly rattled.

In the fifty-sixth minute the match changed completely as Jan Mølby played a slide-rule pass into the Everton area for Rush to race on to before rounding Bobby Mimms and equalising; the watching millions now had a thriller on their hands. Within minutes another Liverpool mix-up at the back resulted in Hansen hoofing a clearance only as far as on onrushing Graeme Sharp at the edge of the penalty area. Sharp was a prodigious header of a ball and he engineered more power with his forehead than many players could with their boots; the ball was thundering to the empty Liverpool net with Grobbelaar stranded. In one of the finest saves any Wembley final has ever witnessed, somehow, quite miraculously really, the keeper raced across his 6-yard box to hurl himself through the air and tip the ball over the crossbar; it was outstanding athleticism and did as much as anything to win the cup for Liverpool.

Within moments of Grobbelaar's save Craig Johnston fired home another Mølby assist. Liverpool had turned a 1-0 deficit to a 2-1 lead within six minutes. With both teams tiring and Everton pressing hard for an equaliser, the game became more stretched as players found more space to play in. Seven minutes from time Ronnie Whelan was in yards of space on the left; he picked out Ian Rush (who had helped start the move 60 yards further back), who controlled the ball with one touch and dispatched it with a second. Rush was like an assassin with a rifle – he just never missed. Many times Everton hearts were broken by the Liverpool number nine, and never did it feel worse for Blues fans than that day. Everton had played so well for so much of the match but still been denied.

The third cup final the two teams contested in five years was the 1989 FA Cup final, but the match and occasion were rightly overshadowed by the events at Hillsborough on 15 April. As the scale of the tragedy became apparent, there was even talk of the cup final not being played that year as a tribute to those who had died. Certainly the idea of business as usual was a non-starter, as the city most affected by the tragedy was once again sending its two sides down to Wembley.

The atmosphere inside the stadium was probably different to any other cup final ever played there; for once, the afternoon's football and the final result were not of paramount importance. Instead, the fact that grieving supporters could come together, almost in tribute to the dead, was much more important than who would go on to win the cup. Football badly needed to be seen in a better light, away from hooliganism, fences and disasters, and that 1989 final represented a couple of tentative first steps along what would be a very long journey to perceived respectability.

The match itself was not as exciting as the '86 final, reflecting the status of the two teams, who were by now probably past their peaks. An early Aldridge goal threatened to be Liverpool's match-winner until Everton substitute Stuart McCall scrambled a late leveller. Further goals were traded in extra time before, almost inevitably. Ian Rush popped up to score the winner. The only real surprise was that Rush's two strikes came from a starting berth on the substitute's bench, a feat unusually matched by Everton's McCall.

Though Liverpool's team danced triumphantly with the trophy, there was a sense that this result somehow mattered less than in other years. Immediately after Hillsborough, football had a million questions to address, and while the sunny afternoon at Wembley told us that the game on the pitch was still in good shape, there remained many issues to resolve.

CAGE FIGHTING

It is pretty undeniable to say that some of the dark moments football reached in the 1980s were as low or lower than almost any other era; decreasing attendances, increasing spectator disorder and three appalling tragedies are testament to those testing times. In those days the match day experience had certain elements which are not missed, but probably should not be forgotten either.

If you travelled as an away fan to any town or city, many assumptions were made about you before you had set foot off any coach or train; firstly, you would need a police escort, complete with horses or even dogs; secondly, sometimes the police might need to use their batons because, as likely as not, trouble would be in the air; lastly, you would be kept in long after the end of the match to minimise the risk of World War Three breaking out on the streets outside. The military-style policing was no fun to be a part of and it was not an edifying spectacle to witness; it antagonised many, but football related violence was no urban myth – there was plenty of it.

Outside of stadiums fans would routinely see Black Maria police vans ready to be filled with felons, CCTV vans were checking everyone's every move and sometimes robust policing could intimidate more than placate. The whole landscape had the feel of some war-torn disaster zone where, if your luck was out, one wrong turn could lead you down the wrong alleyway, at the wrong time, facing the wrong group of opposing fans.

If things were bad enough outside of grounds, the situation in the stadiums was little brighter. Large, ugly spiked fences, like some sort of medieval fortifications, had started to appear in more and more grounds by the end of the 1970s and they quickly became accepted as part of the football environment. It seems strange now, years later, to think that there was no great outcry over the erection of the fences and the penning of fans, as though they were livestock on their way to market. It was seen as a necessary safety measure, the right thing to do if you like. Standing behind the fences was never much fun; your view of the action was obscured and you were left feeling like a criminal. It was sadly true that some fans could not be trusted to simply stand and watch some sport, but whether you were a scrapper or a statto, you were tarred with the same broad stroke of the brush – its indelible imprint simply said 'football fan equals football hooligan'. Football was inhabiting some very bleak times indeed.

ROBSON

In British football in the 1980s, few players came close to Bryan Robson, for stature or for influence. The Manchester United and England captain led by example throughout the decade and was a driving force from his central midfield role. Robson seemed to have everything the modern midfielder needed: he could pass long or short, he could tackle, sometimes like a bulldozer, and he could expertly time runs into opposing penalty areas and score goals.

During his early days, Robson established himself as a key part of Ron Atkinson's exciting West Bromwich Albion team and when Atkinson moved up the M6 to Manchester United, Robson was soon signing on the dotted line on the Old Trafford pitch himself. Quickly establishing himself as the heartbeat of Atkinson's United, he assumed the same mantle with the national team; both sides looked immeasurably more potent when Robson's snarling tackles and raids from midfield were added to the mix.

Although the United teams he played in for most of the decade were not consistently challenging for the league they were mostly a pretty good cup team and it was here that Robson enjoyed most success. In 1983 United met already relegated Brighton in the final and almost fell victim to an almighty upset, Brighton's Gordon Smith famously missed a glorious late chance to win the cup for the Seagulls. United were not so remiss in a replay that Robson dominated; fully justifying his status as the most expensive player in Britain, he scored twice in a 4-0 victory. Shooting home from outside the area and then popping up on the goal line to force home a second, Robson gave a masterclass in attacking from deep.

In 1985 it was Norman Whiteside who hit the headlines at Wembley with a tremendous curling shot to win United a second FA Cup in three years, but it was Robson who had dragged them there. Weeks earlier, in a fiercely-fought semifinal against Liverpool, Robson had once again showcased his attacking verve with the opening goal. A quick exchange of passes by the halfway line with Frank Stapleton saw Robson gallop through the middle of the Liverpool defence before firing into the top corner from over 20 yards' distance; it was inspirational stuff.

Robson enjoyed mixed fortunes on the international stage, playing in the 1982 World Cup and captaining the team for both the 1986 competition and for Euro '88. When fit and injury-free Robson was always a formidable competitor. Manager and namesake Bobby Robson coined the Captain Marvel moniker to salute his number seven's almost superhuman influence. However, the very style of his game meant injuries would inevitably follow; it was impossible to be an all-action player, competing with and confronting opponents for ninety minutes, without suffering collateral damage – and Robson suffered more than his share, with injuries leading to his early departure from both the '86 and '90 World Cups.

The one major prize that eluded Robson for years was the League Championship. The United team he led with such distinction were usually around the top three or four of the league for most of the decade, but they simply could not, as Alex Ferguson famously put it, 'knock Liverpool off their perch.' He would only finally secure a League Championship winner's medal in the twilight of his playing days, well into the 1990s, by which time he had stopped being the first name on the team sheet, and was instead the first name on the substitute's bench. It was during the eighties, though, that Robson stood astride the English game. Talented and fearless in equal measure, he was a marvel of a midfielder with few peers.

DOUBLE DUTCH

After the 1978 World Cup, Tottenham famously brought over two star Argentinians, Ardiles and Villa, to England, and both players almost immediately starred in a successful Spurs team. That move broke the mould in some ways, as it alerted other British teams to the massive player potential that lay outside the British Isles. It took a while, but as the eighties wore on more and more clubs followed Spurs' lead, and the British game would soon become sprinkled with some very fine foreign players.

Ardiles came over with a World Cup winner's medal in his pocket and was truly a coup of a signing. His quicksilver feet, constant movement and love of possession were on another level to what Spurs fans had been used to seeing. Teammate Ricky Villa was tougher, but just as skilful; this was never better seen than in the 1981 Cup Final replay against Manchester City when, like a downhill skier, he slalomed one way and then the other, past everything in his way, before slamming home a glorious winner.

At Portman Road Bobby Robson had spent years assembling a more and more competitive outfit, and after winning the FA Cup in 1978 the next step up was the league. Ipswich went close a couple of times but never quite landed the league championship; they did, however, thrive in European competition and won the 1981 UEFA Cup with a team heavily reliant on two Dutch players, Arnold Mühren and Frans Thijssen. The pair were skilful, they each had a good touch and, crucially in the hurly-burly of the old Division One, they could put their foot on the ball and keep possession – a handy attribute in Europe also.

In the early eighties Liverpool were everyone's rivals and one of their first major foreign singings was a young Zimbabwean, Bruce Grobbelaar, who had impressed during a loan spell at Crewe but had since returned to the NASL with Vancouver Whitecaps. The signing was a massive success as

Grobbelaar stayed for thirteen years, mostly as the first-choice number one, as he wowed crowds with phenomenal agility, athleticism and the shot-stopping ability. Though he was prone to the occasional rush of blood which could take him too far from his line too quickly, you could never amass the number of medals Grobbelaar did without being a consummate goalkeeper. One of his finest hours came in the 1984 European Cup Final in Rome when his famous 'jelly-legs' act in the penalty shoot-out appeared to put Conti and Graziani off, resulting in vital missed penalties. But in truth Grobbelaar had many spectacular moments; at his best he played like he was on springs, bouncing around penalty areas to great effect.

Later, Liverpool supplemented their ranks with other notable overseas players, in particular the speedy and direct Craig Johnson, who scored in the '86 cup final, and another star of the show that day, Denmark's Jan Mølby. Coming from Ajax meant Mølby had received a good schooling before he arrived at Anfield in the summer of 1985, and in his first season he showcased a rare talent. Though never the most athletic-looking of players, the sometimes barrel-chested midfielder played like the conductor of an orchestra; seemingly every movement was directed by him. He could pass short or long, shoot with power and almost never give the ball away. Mølby stayed at Anfield a long time, and though he was not always in the team, whenever he played he had the air of someone playing the game to their very own rhythm – never hurried, never fussed, always highly efficient on the ball.

The increasing success of some of the higher-profile players of course led to more coming through, as English football in particular, started to rely less on the certainties of 4-4-2 formations and its cosy, set ways of doing things. The British game began to open its eyes to other possibilities, and though it would still be years until the likes of Arsène Wenger would come along and revolutionise all aspects of the game, from training regimes to dietary requirements, the winds of change were beginning to gently blow and no part of English football would be untouched.

RED LETTER DAYS

26 FEBRUARY 1983 was the day that Northern Ireland and Arsenal goalkeeper Pat Jennings became the first player to reach 1,000 senior games in British football. Jennings marked the occasion by keeping yet another clean sheet against West Ham, his reflexes and agility showing no signs of being wearied by age.

Jennings started young. He was Watford's first choice at the age of 18, and he memorably played into his 40s, participating in the World Cup finals of 1986 aged 41. He couldn't quite emulate Italy's 40-year-old keeper Dino Zoff by grabbing a winner's medal, but to be still competing with the game's elite at that late stage of his career was phenomenal.

Jennings had all the tools a goalkeeper needed in his kitbag. He had a sound sense of positioning, complemented by an athleticism that enabled him to pull off unlikely saves, and he was blessed with a famously long reach. Jennings could often reach up and pluck the ball from the sky; his party piece was to do so one-handed, towering over forwards like Gulliver in Lilliput. He was fearless and peerless in equal measure.

———

6 NOVEMBER 1986 was to become hugely a pivotal day for Manchester United as it saw both the departure of their manager of the last five years, Ron Atkinson, and the arrival of their manager for the next twenty-six, Alex Ferguson. While many fans and pundits had been predicting Atkinson's demise, few could have guessed at the long-term impact Ferguson would go on to make

In many ways the writing had been on the wall for Atkinson for some time. Despite his two FA Cup wins, his failure to secure a League Championship was being decried by more and more fans. The club was now approaching two full decades since the last triumph. Atkinson had produced good, attractive teams who were more than capable of turning any team over on their day, but they were not quite at the highest level. United never finished lower than fourth under Atkinson, but while that would today bring the kudos and the financial rewards of the Champions League, back then it brought only frustration. Try as they might, United just could not match Liverpool.

In his final season in charge Atkinson's United had started the season like a bullet train, winning their first ten league matches, and it seemed the long wait for that elusive title would soon be ending. Agreeing to sell star striker Mark Hughes to Barcelona halfway through the season did not help the cause and United's form faltered badly; their best chance to be champions in a generation was missed. Still under that cloud when the 1986/87 season opened, Atkinson needed a strong start again, but three straight defeats set the tone for a difficult autumn and by November the board decided he had been given enough time. Atkinson's time at Old Trafford was successful, but for a demanding board and 50,000 fans, it just was not successful enough.

As Atkinson walked out of Old Trafford, ex-Aberdeen manager Alex Ferguson walked through to inherit some talented but now inconsistent players and a huge weight of expectation. Ferguson had already though proved himself to be a winner in Scotland, having broken up Celtic and Rangers' domination of the domestic game with both league titles and cup wins, even having gone on to win the European Cup Winners' Cup. If Atkinson had specialised in producing teams with flair and being a bit of a media darling, Ferguson was the polar opposite – less of the man, and more from the team was what he brought with him.

In his first season, Ferguson could do no more than steady a wobbling ship and acclimatise to the English game. His second year, though, brought discernible progress, as a more consistent United came second to Kenny Dalglish's magnificent team of '88. The progress seemed to stall the following year as a mid-table finish was all that was achieved amid murmurings about the departures of one-time leading men Paul McGrath and Norman Whiteside. By the end of the decade the murmurings became

more pronounced as United struggled to impose themselves in the league. But though nobody knew it at the
time, salvation was just around the corner. An FA Cup triumph in 1990 kick-started the Ferguson era, and within just a
year or two of the new decade starting Ferguson was having to
make a regular order for the trophy cabinet to be extended as
United would go on to dominate the nineties as their great rivals
Liverpool had dominated the seventies and eighties.

---

9 MAY 1987 saw one of the strangest tales to emerge from the
lower reaches of the Football League for years. For Division Four
clubs the safety net of the re-election process had been finally
dispensed with and it was the first year of automatic relegation from the Fourth Division to the Conference – a terrifying
prospect for Torquay United who were battling with Lincoln to
avoid the drop. United needed to get something from their final
fixture at home to Crewe, but with time running out it was the
Alex who led 2-1 and the trapdoor out of the professional game
was being made ready for Torquay. When United's Jim McNichol
went down injured for a routine pause, something quite extraordinary happened – a police dog called Ginger took an interest in
the prostrate McNichol and, abandoning all police dog training
protocol and etiquette, decided to quite literally take a bite.

After first writhing in considerable discomfort, McNichol was
then treated on the pitch, forcing a delay in the action of about five
minutes. Towards the end of the additional five minutes United's
Paul Dobson popped up with an equaliser that preserved his teams'
league status and sent down Lincoln City on goal difference. In
return for the part that Ginger the dog played in the narrowest of
squeaks, Torquay's Chairman, a man called Pope, promised Ginger
the largest of steaks, though how hungry he still was after feasting
on the Torquay full back, was never quite established.

---

10 JULY 1988 became a day of huge significance in Scottish football, and for Glasgow Rangers Football Club in particular, as it was the day that Rangers, for the first time in their history, signed a Catholic player, Mo Johnston, from French side Nantes. Manger Graeme Souness had been at Ibrox for three highly successful years already and had previously declared he would not hesitate to sign Catholics if he saw fit to; he was himself married to a Catholic and his only criteria was footballing ability. Saying it and doing it, though, were two entirely different matters for sections of the Rangers support.

It is hard to imagine now, almost three decades on, but some supporters were so incensed by the move that demonstrations were held outside Ibrox Park, with scarves, programmes and tickets being burnt in protest at the move. For decades Rangers had prided themselves on being a Protestant club for Protestant fans, and the change Souness was introducing had a massive impact; belatedly, the club would be dragged into the twentieth century, in which tolerance was a strength not a weakness. Johnston's signing was an unmistakeable signal that the days of bigotry and of choosing players on the basis of their religious convictions rather than their footballing talents were to be challenged and rejected.

Souness often played, sometimes even managed, a bit like an erupting volcano, his head was hotter than most, but on this occasion his actions spoke louder than any words; his leadership made the most eloquent case for tolerance and he effected some long overdue and necessary change.

---

18 JANUARY 1989 was a day that a couple of Nottingham Forest fans will probably never forget, as on that night that Nottingham Forest manager Brian Clough took the law firmly into his own hands and walloped the pair for going on to the pitch at the end of a League Cup quarter-final win against

Queens Park Rangers. The discipline he famously insisted upon from his own teams was strangely absent from his own behaviour that night.

The evening itself had been a great success for Forest, with five goals scored and a semi-final place booked. Forest fans, filled with good humour, encroached on to the playing area at the end of the match to celebrate what looked like a return to the big time for Forest after some relatively modest top-flight years. Clough though, was having none of the bonhomie football fans feel like sharing on such occasions, and he decided to make his point in short, sharp and succinct fashion – he 'clipped the ears', or punched if you prefer, two of the closest celebrating fans and marched them off the pitch. Clough was admired by some for making his point and tackling the pitch invaders, others though were critical of him descending to some pretty unsavoury behaviour himself. The following day Clough apologised for his actions and soon afterwards he was apologising to the fans too, explaining that he had acted with the best of intentions but in the wrong way.

Despite his apologies, Clough was punished by the FA but managed to keep a hold of his job; he was fined £5,000 and received a touchline ban for the rest of the season. Curiously, within days the two fans were visiting Clough, whereupon he made them kiss him to indicate his forgiveness of them for going on to the pitch! It is doubtful that any other manager working in the English game at that time would have done what Clough did in the first place, never mind gone on to dispense his own forgiveness as though he was some sort of infallible Pope figure. Clough was rightly regarded as an original and maverick manager even touched by greatness, but on this occasion he certainly crossed a line that was best left well alone.

HAIR TODAY

For the more hirsute footballers, the 1980s was a decade to simply let nature – or blonde highlights and the hairdryer – take its natural course. Of course haircuts come in all shapes and sizes, and for every David Armstrong there was, perhaps, a George Berry, but the 1980s was unmistakably a time of big statements and some pretty big hair too.

While it seemed the era offered something for everyone, some players appearances are harder to forget (and forgive), no matter how hard we try to. Take, for instance, the immaculately coiffured Barry Venison of Sunderland and Liverpool. Unafraid and unabashed, Venison seemed to have the lot: a feather cut, a blow-dry and a mullet, all on one head, all at the same time. Whether the north-easterner represented a triumph of post-modern masculinity or, as some away supporters could suggest, a bit of a softy, is open to ongoing conjecture.

Less open to debate is the role of Coventry cup-winning skipper Brian Kilcline in bringing the simple hair follicle into disrepute. Kilcline's gory locks represented his style of play – more agricultural than conditioned and more Viking than city chic. Killer's hair resembled nothing more than a marauding plunderer, perilously close to combusting if just one more speedy striker left him for dead. Like thousands of Norsemen before him, Kilcline's ever-lengthening hair, could not hide his murderous intent.

THE NUMBERS GAME

Some more stats that add-up...

11 was the number of games England cricket all-rounder Ian Botham played in the Football League for Scunthorpe United in the 1980s. While the idea of any modern-day centrally contracted Test player swapping their cricket spikes for football boots is pretty much unthinkable, when Botham achieved the distinction he was continuing a tradition that went back decades. Arsenal winger Dennis Compton was the best of the bunch, winning the league in 1948 and the FA Cup in 1950 as well as hitting seventeen Test centuries. Botham's Test-match pedigree was just as impressive, with fourteen centuries and 383 Test wickets, but his physical, rugged style of defending was only seen in the lower leagues.

30 matches was the number of league games it took Manchester United striker Garry Birtles to finally score a league goal after his £1.25 million move from Nottingham Forest to Old Trafford. Birtles had enjoyed great success at the City Ground, winning two European Cups and a League Cup medal while scoring fifty goals in a little over two seasons. He was rightly considered one of England's top strikers at the time of the move to Manchester but, aside from a solitary FA Cup strike, no matter how hard he tried he simply could not score. Birtles took eleven months to break his league duck, before finally hitting some form and going on to reach double figures for the season. Within two years of leaving Nottingham he returned to Forest in a cut-price transfer, where he went on to score regularly once again, leaving the Old Trafford faithful puzzled as to what exactly had afflicted him on the bigger stage.

7 was the number of consecutive seasons that the League Championship went to Merseyside. From 1982–88, first Liverpool with a hat-trick of triumphs and then Everton with two of their own dominated the domestic scene. The red and blue halves of Liverpool fielded pacey, attractive teams who were able to put long winning runs together, while the rest of the country could not quite break their stranglehold.

SAY HELLO, WAVE GOODBYE

The Mexico World Cup in 1986 gave us many things to savour: Maradona's skills, Lineker's golden boot, Negrete's balletic volley for the host nation against Bulgaria, but aside from the action on the pitch it gave us the phenomenon that would go on to be dubbed the Mexican Wave. When large sections in the stadium stand up in unison and raise both arms aloft you have a wave, and of course it being in Mexico meant it was the Mexican wave. Historians of such things (who arguably need to get out more) dispute the origins of the wave. Some point to the Los Angeles Olympics in 1984 as the starting point, others suggest it debuted at major league baseball or even the Mexican domestic football league years, or even decades earlier. No matter really, the wave came to prominence during the '86 tournament and has since been adopted and copied in stadiums around the world.

The basic premise is unchanging; everyone stands up for a few seconds, throws their arms around and makes an almighty noise, before the wave departs for the next block in the stand. A universal feature almost across the world, though, seems to be the reluctance of those fans seated in the most expensive seats to join in. No matter how aesthetically pleasing or fulsome the wave might be, time and time again it simply dissipates when it runs aground on the stony faces of the corporate gang.

The idea that fun at football could have a socio–economic correlation might be one for the sociologists. In the meantime, though, if you are at a match sometime soon and the action has slowed a little, get ready for the flailing arms, the crescendo of noise and the feeling of being part of something greater than yourself as you give the players a giant nod to get on and make the match a bit more worth watching!

GOALS OF THE SEASON:

1979/80
Justin Fashanu
Carrow Road, First Division, February 1980
Norwich City 3 Liverpool 5

At the time of this memorable strike Justin Fashanu seemed to have all the attributes for a significant top-flight career; he was muscular, quick and possessed a powerful shot. That combination was never better illustrated than in this exquisite turn, flick up and arrowing shot into the top right-hand side of Ray Clemence's net. In a career, and life, that was to often be more complicated than Fashanu would have wanted, this goal stands testament to the fantastic potential he showed as a young player, when simply turning your man and lashing in from 25 yards was what you did, because you could.

1980/81
Tony Morley
Goodison Park, First Division, February 1981
Everton 1 Aston Villa 3

The spring of 1981 was a golden time for everyone connected with Aston Villa as their attacking team pipped Ipswich to the title by just four points. Villa famously won the league after fielding only fourteen players all season, with left-winger Tony Morley a crucial part of their attacking arsenal. Morley could run with the ball at pace and wrong-foot defenders in a flash, and at Goodison Park he was simply too quick to handle. Collecting a smart through-ball from Gary Shaw, Morley galloped down the left wing before cutting in to hit a rising shot with his preferred right foot. The winger himself almost took off as he launched the ball from just outside the Everton box, leaving Villa fans delirious as their first title for seventy-one years slowly came into view.

1981/82
Cyrille Regis
The Hawthorns, FA Cup, February 1982
West Bromwich Albion 1 Norwich City 0

Over almost two decades in the professional game Cyrille Regis was a defender's nightmare. He had brutal strength, adhesive control and, a bit like satnav today, an unfailing awareness of what was going on around him. In this fifth-round cup tie Regis gave a mini masterclass in the art of being a striker. Close to the centre circle, with his back to goal, he expertly collected the ball on his chest before turning two defenders and striding for goal. Without hesitation, from close to 30 yards out he propelled the ball at pace into the top left-hand corner of the net before any defender could get close to him. This was Regis at his best, both purposeful and powerful – a magnificent centre forward.

1982/83
Kenny Dalglish
Heysel Stadium, European Championship Qualifier, December 1982
Belgium 3 Scotland 2

In the days when Scotland were regulars at World Cup Finals, they boasted some top-quality names on their team sheets. While McLeish and Hansen shored up the back, with Strachan and Souness patrolling and prompting from mid-field, it was up front that the Scots had their brightest light, in three-time European Cup winner, Kenny Dalglish. A glittering career with Celtic became the warm-up at for a decade of dazzling forward play with the all-conquering Liverpool in which Dalglish was always both a creator and taker of chances. In a fiercely contested qualifier in Belgium Dalglish's early dash put Scotland ahead, and just after half an hour he was at it again. Collecting the ball on the right-hand corner of the penalty area, his deft right foot killed the ball instantly, allowing him to turn his man. Effortlessly switching, at pace, from right to left foot, Dalglish then curled a beauty into the top corner of Belgium's net, showcasing in seconds what many strikers could not do in a whole career – how to make and take your own chances.

1983/84
Danny Wallace
The Dell, Division One, March 1984
Southampton 2 Liverpool 0

The Southampton side of 1984 secured their highest ever league position, finishing second in the league just three points away from champions Liverpool. The Saints team was a mixture of all sorts and all ages, experience in abundance, with Mick Mills, Frank Worthington and England's Peter Shilton, was complemented by some fast-emerging younger talents like Mark Wright and the nippy forward Danny Wallace. Mark Wright started the move deep inside his own half and after swift exchanges down the left side Mark Dennis's cross looped down to Wallace, who stood with his back to goal. In the split second he had, Wallace instinctively produced a bicycle kick of the rarest technique, straight out of the coaching books and into the roof of the bamboozled Bruce Grobbelaar's net, for a goal even Matt Le Tissier would have been proud of.

1984/85
Graeme Sharp
Anfield, Division One, October 1984
Liverpool 0 Everton 1

If ever a goal signalled a changing of the guard, it was perhaps Graeme Sharp's thunderbolt into the Anfield Road goal in the 131st Merseyside Derby. Liverpool had been domestic champions for three successive seasons and once again were European Cup holders; Everton by contrast were an emerging team, fresh their own FA Cup triumph, and looking like they might be able to threaten Liverpool's supremacy for the first time in over a decade. When Gary Stevens played a lengthy first-time ball into the centre of Liverpool's defence, hopes would not have been particularly high, since Lawrenson and Hansen hoovered up most opposing forwards between them. This time, though, Sharp's intelligent running in between the Liverpool central defenders made a yard or two of space, which he cashed in on in spectacular style. Taking the ball with his left foot, he let it bounce once before, in true Roy Race style, rocketing the ball past Bruce Grobbelaar from 25 yards. Thirty years on, Sharp's goal is still fondly remembered in the blue half of Liverpool as the moment Everton announced their arrival as serious contenders once again, in a season that was to bring European glory and their first domestic championship since 1970.

1985/86
Bryan Robson
Tel Aviv, International Friendly, February 1986
Israel 1 England 2

In the spring of 1986 there were some things you could rely on in English football: the title would be won by a team from Merseyside, when Ian Rush scored Liverpool would never lose and when Bryan Robson was fully fit and firing he would win most of his midfield scraps. When he was at his peak throughout the eighties, there were few midfielders who could reach Robson's levels of midfield athleticism, touch and inspiration. Captain Marvel, as Bobby Robson christened the England captain, was simply something special. Robson's equalising goal against Israel in 1986 was typical of the player. Showing great awareness in timing a forward-thinking run, Robson found a yard of space in the penalty area and calmly scissored a volley into the top corner of the Israel net. Understanding of when to arrive in the penalty area was as much a feature of the England captain's game as the heavy-duty tackle and slide-rule pass, and it was this combination that served Manchester United and England well for over a decade as Robson tore up and down pitches to great effect.

1986/87
Keith Houchen
Wembley Stadium, FA Cup Final, May 1987
Coventry City 3 Tottenham Hotspur 2

If the term is not too pejorative to use in polite conversation, it can pretty safely be said that when Keith Houchen arrived at Coventry's Highfield Road in the summer of 1986 he was a journeyman striker. His early promise at Hartlepool United seemed to have petered out after unremarkable spells at Orient, York City and Scunthorpe, and by the time Coventry came calling, Houchen had looked most likely to be set for a life trawling the lower leagues. Like many players plying their trade out of the spotlight though, Houchen had not so much lacked ability as the opportunity to show that ability. At Coventry he got and took that opportunity. Strong in the air, able to hold the ball up well and good for a goal or two, Houchen had enough in his arsenal to hurt teams, and, on a sunny afternoon at Wembley, he hurt Tottenham Hotspur. In an open game that ebbed and flowed both ways, Coventry found themselves pressing for an equaliser in the second-half. Skyscraper keeper Ogrizovic launched a high ball for Cyrille Regis to flick on to Houchen, who smartly found wide man Dave Bennett, before turning on his heels and heading to the centre of the penalty box. Bennett's in-swinging cross evaded the Spurs defenders and, like a waiting assassin, Houchen simply took aim and fired. With his whole body airborne, the Coventry number ten made the sweetest of contacts to steer the ball past Clemence into the net. As Houchen defied gravity, so had Coventry defied logic, and soon the cup would need some new sky-blue ribbons.

1987/88
John Aldridge
Hillsborough, FA Cup Semi-final, April 1988
Liverpool 2 Nottingham Forest 1

The goal that won the 1988 award was conceived a year before, when Everton had had the audacity to steal Liverpool's title for the second time in three years. Liverpool manager Kenny Dalglish, still a nominal player-manager, knew as his legs were ageing that his team needed refreshing and he came up with a plan. Three eye-catching strikers, Peter Beardsley, John Aldridge and John Barnes became an expensively assembled new forward line, who, in their first season together produced a vintage red all of their own. The new men each had their own distinct contributions to make: Beardsley provided the nous, Barnes the verve and thrust, and Aldridge an unerring eye for goal. In characteristic fashion the three combined superbly in the cup semi-final to double Liverpool's lead. Collecting a long ball from defence Beardsley, exchanged perfectly weighted passes with Barnes before setting the wide man free down the Forest left flank. The first-time cross from Barnes was acrobatically volleyed home by the advancing Aldridge, the man who made the impossible job of replacing Ian Rush look easy. As for much of the year, Liverpool's skill and speed simply left their opponents static and trailing; it was exhibition football on the highest stage.

1988/89
John Aldridge
Wembley Stadium, FA Cup Final, May 1989
Liverpool 3 Everton 2

The facts of the goal are straight-forward enough to relate: a Steve Nicol through ball, a nimble touch from Steve McMahon and an assured side-footer from Liverpool's number nine, John Aldridge, into the top corner of Neville Southall's net; it was a goal typical of a fine Liverpool side – incisive, speedy and skilfully finished. For a first scene in a drama, it was heady stuff, and despite a period of quiet the final provided plenty of further exhilaration in its closing stages, before inevitably being settled by Ian Rush. However, the cup final of 1989 can never be thought of for its' footballing merits alone. It was played just over a month after the Hillsborough Disaster; perhaps never before had a match meant more to a city and never before had the result of a match mattered less.

DAVID v. GOLIATH: LIVERPOOL 0 WIMBLEDON 1, 1988

The 1988 FA Cup Final between Liverpool and Wimbledon show-cased one of the competition's enduring strengths: the chance for a lowly underdog to knock a high-flying outfit off their lofty perch. The chance for the romance of the cup to reassert itself.

In the red corner were the all-conquering Liverpool; a club with a decades-long tradition of winning major prizes. That year, under Kenny Dalglish's stewardship, they had taken their play to a whole new level. Supplemented by three stellar signings in Aldridge, Beardsley and Barnes, they had become an almost irresistible attacking force, going twenty-nine games unbeaten from the start of the year. It seemed no one could lay a glove on them.

In the blue corner were Wimbledon, a club who called ram-shackle Plough Lane home, who had only ten years earlier been plying their trade outside of the football league. The Dons tradition was of hard-scrapped-for promotions, plenty of physical effort and a direct, in-your-face, confrontational style. The contrast could not have been greater, if Liverpool were a Rolls-Royce of a team, smoothly and smartly outmanoeuvring all comers, Wimbledon were more like a JCB, bulldozing their way around Division One.

The contrast was summed up neatly in the opposing manag-ers. Liverpool's Dalglish had spent a decade at Anfield winning everything on the pitch before shaping an expansive, progressive team who, under his stewardship, had continued to dominate. Meanwhile, Wimbledon's Bobby Gould had completed his mana-gerial apprenticeship at Bristol Rovers and Coventry City, where he had gained plenty of experience of close scrapes, but none of trophy-lifting. The clubs, the managers and the players were not so much poles apart, then, as galaxies.

Of course heritage and history are fine things, but when the referee Brian Hill blew his whistle for kick-off, backstories counted for nothing on the pitch. How little they mattered was seen after just nine minutes when Wimbledon's Vinny Jones, not known for his deference, set the tone by simply scything Steve McMahon down, almost splitting him in two in the process, with no regard for the ball. To his credit, McMahon got straight up and didn't flinch, but Jones had left the mother of all calling cards; if Liverpool's ability could be trumped by appetite or outright aggression, Wimbledon had a chance.

Liverpool began brightly, and just after half an hour Beardsley rode an Andy Thorn challenge to fire past keeper Beasant. However, referee Hill had already blown for a foul and, controversially, no advantage was played – the goal did not stand. If Wimbledon were lucky then, there was no good fortune about what happened minutes later. A smartly-flighted free-kick from Dennis Wise was expertly deflected into the Liverpool net by Lawrie Sanchez – the Dons had the lead just before half-time.

The very thing that pundits and punters alike had said could not happen was slowly unfolding before the nation – Wimbledon were leading and threatening an almighty cup final shock. Liverpool had forty-five minutes to put things right and when they were awarded a penalty after an hour, things seemed set to fall into their expected place. John Aldridge had scored all eleven penalties he had taken that season, but he could not make it twelve as Dave Beasant threw himself to his left to push the ball away, becoming the first goalkeeper to save a penalty in an FA Cup final.

Though Liverpool continued to enjoy possession, and to press and probe they could not find a way through a rugged, physical Wimbledon, who simply refused to be breached. As the final whistle signalled an improbable Wimbledon victory, the glorious unpredictability of the FA Cup was once again there for all to see. Liverpool's extravagant talents had been undone by Wimbledon's more prosaic players, and as BBC commentator John Motson famously declared, 'the Crazy Gang have beaten the Culture Club' – he had a point.

CALL FOR MR PLUMLEY

When Watford ambushed Arsenal in the 1986/87 FA Cup Quarter-final at Highbury, Graham Taylor's men were just ninety minutes away from a second cup final in four years. Although semi-final opponents Tottenham were enjoying a fine season of attacking play them, the Hornets had plenty of sting of their own, with John Barnes and Luther Blissett prominent.

Most pundits thought Watford would need a slice or two of good luck to turn over Tottenham, but in the build-up to the semi-final the only fortune Watford had was the wretched bad luck which upsets even the best-laid plans. While regular keeper Tony Coton was out with a broken finger, his back-up, Steve Sherwood, was a time-served and capable deputy, having himself played in the 1984 final. The idea was for Sherwood to deputise, but things were about to get tricky for Taylor's men.

Rather than risk a talented, but untested 16-year-old called David James as the sub keeper, Watford sought an emergency back-up and Chief Executive Eddie Plumley had a plan. Plumley's son Gary was a recently retired professional keeper, now working outside of the game – he owned a wine bar. While at work, he took a call from his father inviting him to train with Watford and to be their substitute keeper for the semi-final. The plan was for Plumley to be nowhere near the action; the plan backfired.

When Steve Sherwood dislocated a finger in training, the only credible option was to install Plumley between the sticks and hope for the best. Plumley played, but Watford didn't seem to, and a little after half an hour they trailed 3-0, with their dreams of Wembley dashed. Though the keeper might possibly have done better with a couple of the goals, Watford were convincingly beaten. After the match Watford went on to finish ninth, Tottenham went on to lose a thrilling final to Coventry City and Plumley simply went back to his wine bar and never played another professional match.

GOAL IN ONE

Since the start of the Premier League each goal scored by every player, in all games, has been routinely emblazoned across the airwaves and the Information Superhighway within seconds – how times have changed over thirty years. Previously, when the most spectacular or improbable of goals was scored it could often only be replayed in the minds of the spectators who witnessed it live, which was very good news for embarrassed goalkeepers everywhere, particularly if they had been caught out by their opposite number.

At Coventry City's former Highfield Road stadium, on an arctic January afternoon in 1984, the perennially struggling Sky Blues had been enjoying life in the top half of Division One. Just a month previously they had walloped reigning champions Liverpool 4-0 and the ragtag team of lower leaguers was exceeding all expectations; the visit of struggling Watford brought high hopes, but also high winds.

City's one-cap Yugoslavian keeper, Raddy Avramović, had had a quiet opening ten minutes or so as the game coasted along, not yet out of first gear. Watford's dependable number one, Steve Sherwood, routinely collected the ball and then seemingly paused for a moment's reflection. Quite what it is that keeper's consider as they clutch the ball to their chests has always been unclear. Perhaps Sherwood was contemplating the nuances and subtleties of Graham Taylor's tactics; perhaps, like former Sky Blue keeper David Icke, he was considering which reptilian bloodlines ruled the world; or perhaps he was simply looking forward to his tea. Whatever was on his mind, Sherwood's pause was critical as it allowed the winds around the stadium to merge and converge above the penalty area of the West Terrace goal; as the ball was then hoofed skywards it seemed to take on a trajectory all of its own, soaring steeply, before bouncing, menacingly, on the edge of Coventry's penalty area.

City's keeper Avramović was a former law student, but he cannot have covered the laws of physics too closely, as he horribly misjudged the startling bounce and was left floored as the ball gently bobbled into the empty net. Avramović's error was costly on the day, as Coventry slipped to a narrow defeat. Within weeks, manager Bobby Gould publicly declared his patience was at an end and that Raddy would never play for him again – which he did not.

Almost three years later, Coventry were involved again in a goalkeeper stealing all the headlines for their goal-scoring prowess. By the winter of 1986 the ex-policeman Steve Ogrizovic was patrolling the Coventry net to great effect. The BFG of goalkeepers was forging a strong reputation as a reliable and athletic number one; he had not hitherto been noted for his shooting.

Sheffield Wednesday's Hillsborough stadium was the miserable setting for a Division One fixture that was played in appalling conditions. As the rain and wind lashed the players, Ogrizovic had a simple theory that he had been patiently waiting to test out. During the week City's number one had been discussing how his opposite number, Wednesday's Martin Hodge, tended to sometimes stray a long way from his goal and could be susceptible to a giant clearance. All big Oggy needed was the wind at his back and a bit of good fortune.

After just over an hour's play and with the sides locked together at 1-1, Ogrizovic clasped the ball firmly in both hands, peered towards the giant Hillsborough Kop and saw Hodge a little off his line. From his own penalty-spot Ogrizovic launched an almighty, steepling punt towards Hodge's goal and two bounces later the ball nestled itself in the Wednesday net via Hodge's right-hand post.

Although the Hillsborough wind certainly assisted Ogrizovic, he deserved credit for having planned to take a punt on Hodge's positioning if the weather conditions were in his favour. Typical of the man, Oggy remained modest afterwards, preferring to downplay his strategic thinking, and in true goalkeepers union style he even commiserated with Hodge. In total, Ogrizovic went on to play 601 first team games for the Sky Blues; many times he saved them from relegation scrapes, but he never again found the net.

MOMENT IN TIME: MARCO VAN BASTEN, 1988

The Dutch team of 1988 were highly fancied before they even set foot in Germany. Their squad had serious quality running through it with the likes of Rijkaard, Koeman, Mühren, van Basten and European Player of the year Ruud Gullit. The big question was whether they could keep things together for a whole tournament and finally shake off the bridesmaid's tag they had gained by losing in two successive World Cup Finals ten years before. Back in charge of the squad was the manager of the splendid 1974 team, Rinus Michels, one of the architects of the Total Football philosophy, a style in which positions were less rigidly adhered to and players' movement was much more fluid. With Michels back at the helm and the array of talent he had to work with, the Dutch looked strong.

They opened slowly with a 1-0 reverse against the Soviet Union, but from thereon they started to show what they could do. Van Basten served notice of his deadliness in front of goal with a brilliant hat-trick against England, which sent Bobby Robson's men packing, leaving the match against the Republic of Ireland as a de facto quarter-final. Holland came within minutes of elimination as the Republic scrapped all the way, but a slightly fortuitous Wim Kieft goal clinched it for the Dutch sending them to Hamburg to take on a West German side they had not beaten for thirty-two years. With the game tied at 1-1 and only moments remaining, Wouters threaded a ball into the penalty area where, without breaking stride, Van Basten raced on and hooked the ball low into the right-hand corner of Immel's net. Almost regardless of the final, for Holland this was revenge for the '74 defeat and the path to redemption was now clear – only the Soviets stood in their way.

Most observers thought the Dutch had too much for the Russians before the final and in some ways the game became straightforward for them. A thumping header from Gullit just after half an hour underlined the Dutch sharpness in front of goal; if that goal was clever, their second was simply celestial. Van Tiggelen carried the ball forward before sliding it to the left flank where veteran Mühren arced a deep cross over the back-peddling defenders, towards the right-hand edge of the penalty area. Van Basten was just about in line with the 6-yard box when, for the split second it took to connect with the ball, both his feet were in mid-air; he connected perfectly, firing goalwards despite the impossible angle, and, like a tracer bullet from a machine gun, the ball flew unstoppably and unerringly into the roof of the net. If Bobby Charlton, Diego Maradona and even Roy Race had combined, they could not have hit a better volley, from a less likely place. The goal capped a sublime tournament for lead scorer Van Basten, and for a time, before injuries defeated him, he was capable of both the most brilliant thought and the most brilliant execution; Total Football from the total striker.

ELECTRIC DREAMS

There is simply no point in trying to escape certain facts about football in the mid 1980s. Even before the desperately sad tragedies of Bradford, Heysel or Hillsborough, football was in an increasingly parlous state. Attendances had started to reduce sharply; in 1977, some 26 million people watched football, yet by 1983 that figure had dropped to just under 19 million. But the calamity of losing a quarter of all customers in three years was not the only concern. Spectator disorder was becoming more and more prominent also, with 1985 seeing appalling riots during televised games at both Chelsea and Luton. The decreasing attendances and increasing crowd disorder made for a toxic mix, and many declared, from both within and outside of the sport, that some things needed to change. One such declarative voice belonged to the then chairman of Chelsea, the characteristically outspoken Ken Bates. Like many others, when Bates decried the state of spectator conduct, he had a point; unlike almost all others, though, his point was a bit like the one you find at the tip of a compass – it was sharp, it was spiky and it could be used aggressively.

Stamford Bridge had seen some appalling scenes during a 1985 Milk Cup semi-final against Sunderland as fans fought on the pitch while police horses tried to restore order. Bates' reaction to try to do something to stem the trouble sounded plausible enough for several sentences, but only until he explained how he planned to install a 12ft-high electric fence along the whole of the pitch. Bates reasoned that the possibility of receiving a 12-volt shock would dissuade spectators from going anywhere near the pitch. He seemed to forget that people attending a form of entertainment should not necessarily be treated like animals or criminals or, for that matter, electrocuted. London's GLC ordered the fence to be removed days before the fence was due to make its debut against Tottenham, and Bates never got to turn on his switch.

Years later, the story is now no more than a footnote in the litany of answers to football hooliganism, but from the prism of the Premier League era it is interesting to reflect on just how little had come to be thought of spectators.

DARKEST DAYS, 1989

On 15 April 1989, for the second year running Nottingham Forest and Liverpool, met in the FA Cup semi-final at Sheffield Wednesday's Hillsborough stadium. What should have been another fantastic footballing occasion, shared by two skilful teams driven by their inspirational mangers Clough and Dalglish, can only ever be remembered for the tragic events that led to ninety-six football fans losing their lives.

The previous year, when Liverpool had won 2-1, their fans had filled the larger end of the ground, the enormous Hillsborough Kop, and the game had passed without incident; twelve months later things were very different. This time around the larger Liverpool support was given the smaller Leppings Lane End to fill. The congregating crowds were not effectively cordoned into waiting lines outside the stadium, and, fearful of a crush outside the ground, the police opened the stadium gates. This fateful decision, perhaps well-intentioned, but surely made in panic, had calamitous consequences. Hundreds of fans, anxious not to miss kick-off, poured into an already brim-full central pen, while pens to both the left and right were not filled. Either better signposting or effective stewarding would have funnelled the arriving fans into safe areas; neither was present. A dreadful, life-sapping crush developed. Just six minutes after kick-off the game was halted, as it became clear that there was a major problem on the terrace. The problem was compounded by the security fences that fringed the terraces; their presence meant the very fans who were being crushed had no means of escape. Eventually, the lives of ninety-six people, who happened to be football fans, were ended that afternoon at Hillsborough.

Now more than a generation has passed since Hillborough, and its consequences continue to resonate. Shamefully, the bereaved families unbearable pain was exacerbated by being made to wait three full decades before receiving the whole sorry truth of the afternoon and its aftermath. Unlike the families, who were given a life sentence of loss, football was given a second chance. As the FA Chairman of the time, Graham Kelly, succinctly put it, 'things have to change'; *The Sunday Times* labelled football as a 'slum sport played in slum stadiums' in 1989. They were both right. The Taylor Report investigated the disaster and called for seismic changes in the national game; most pivotally, terraces were to be outlawed in favour of more sanitised, all-seated, but safer stadiums; football's squalid conditions were finally to be consigned to the history books.

MAKING PLANS FOR NIGEL

When Aston Villa's reserve keeper Nigel Spink took his place as one of Villa's five substitutes for their 1982 European Cup Final showdown against Bayern Munich, he was the least experienced of the back-ups. Having played just one solitary first team match some two and a half years earlier, Spink seemed to be putting the rook into rookie.

With experienced number one Jimmy Rimmer in situ, Spink settled down to enjoy the best seat in the house. But not ten minutes after kick-off Rimmer's suspect shoulder led to his early exit and Spinks' gloves were on; the Villa reserve was tasked with repelling Germany's finest, including Breitner, Augenthaler and Rummenigge.

If Spinks felt nervous he never showed it; almost immediately picking up a misplaced Bayern pass to get an early touch, he went on to play with the assurance of a veteran. Some early first half saves displayed immaculate handling and when Karl-Heinz Rummenigge cut in from the edge of the penalty area to fire a ferocious drive low to Spinks' left, the number sixteen athletically pushed it away.

After Peter Withe shinned the opening goal a little after an hour, the pressure on Villa's rearguard grew, yet Spinks grew in stature and, one clearly offside goal apart, Munich simply could not find a way past him. What started out as a potential nightmare for Villa and their young novice reserve turned into an unbelievable triumph, rising to the greatest of occasions, holding his nerve and finally holding the cup aloft.

Spinks went on to play a further 459 times for the men in claret and blue, but despite nineteen years of sterling service it is fair to say his finest footballing achievement came in just his second outing, when, like in an A-ha video, the comic-strip kid became a real-life hero.

THE THINGS THEY SAY

The Sky Blues are sky high.

John Motson, BBC

FA Cup Final, May 1987
Coventry City 3 Tottenham Hotspur 2
As Coventry City skipper Brian Kilcline raised the trophy to the heavens, he signalled the end of Coventry's 104-year wait for a major trophy. In the commentary box, John Motson momentarily let his statesman-like stance slip and simply inhaled the Sky Blue euphoria before exhaling his catchy little phrase, so well-liked in the West Midlands that almost three decades later they're still replaying the line at home matches.

TWO BECOME ONE

In 1983 the good football folk of Oxford and Reading received quite a shock with the announcement that Oxford owner Robert Maxwell was giving serious thought into trying to merge the two clubs to become the Thames Valley Royals. Traditionally both teams had been lower-league out-fits, seldom threatening the higher divisions, but with high aspirations for their own futures; those aspirations naturally extended to seeing their own clubs rise up the pyramid, as Oxford so memorably managed to as the decade went on.

Maxwell's thinking was pragmatism at its purest – simply take two moderately successful clubs, mix them up together, double the fan base in an instant and see if you can't churn out a club to rival the big boys in London and up north – instant gratification for everyone. Quite rightly, most football clubs spend years charting a future pathway, incrementally and meticulously foreseeing every opportunity and hurdle they might meet on their journey. Maxwell's plan however, appeared to be more from the back-of-a-matchbox school of thought; he simply did not take into account the people who might be most affected by the seismic change – the fans.

Opinions on Maxwell varied; some (himself included) had him down as a football visionary, prepared to defy convention and turn years of staid tradition on its head in search of a brighter future. Others though thought less charitably of his plans and considered his apparent lack of understanding of fan identity and culture as frightening; he simply did not get the fact that Oxford fans wanted to follow Oxford and that Reading fans wanted to follow Reading.

The franchise idea, of uprooting and creating teams anew, had always been anathema to English fans, who based their allegiances on clear certainties – Oxford play in Oxford, probably always in yellow, and often down the leagues, but that's Oxford – they are not, never have been and never will be Manchester United! While the game must develop and evolve, there are some things, like teams identities that are probably best left to simply endure. If football fans cannot rely on immutable facts of existence then trouble lies ahead; ask the Cardiff fans, who saw their shirt colour change from traditional blue to red to suit far-eastern marketing, or the Coventry City fans, whose home changed from Coventry to Northampton to suit hedge fund owners who did not want to pay their rent. Of course, the modern era has its fit and proper owners tests to ensure such things do not occur and then occur again and again and again!

Maxwell himself was not pleased by the hostility to his plans. Perhaps unused to being refused, he saw the backlash as a slight. He was an interesting character with varied interests; he had been an MP, he was a successful publisher and he owned a national newspaper. In some ways he was a forerunner for the cult of modern owners: foreign-born, very wealthy and yet perhaps not fully embracing the richness of fan culture that English football engenders. Whether Maxwell was a visionary or a villain, Oxford and Reading continue to ply their lonely furrows alone, very much enjoying their own occasional successes, long after Maxwell's plans to merge the two sank without trace.

SUDDEN DEATH

As the 1982 World Cup finals reached the semi-final, four European teams, Poland, Italy, France and West Germany, were left battling for a place in the final. In the first semi, Italy managed to dispatch Poland in fairly straightforward style, 2-0, thanks to two goals from born-again Paolo Rossi. The second semi-final, contested that same evening in Seville, would be anything but a clear-cut affair.

West Germany had got to the last four despite quite an unhappy tournament; an early shock defeat to Algeria was followed by a final group match in which they openly colluded with Austria to manipulate the game. The world's scorn showered down upon the German team after that episode, but the reigning European champions, just got on with getting through the rounds. Although that year's vintage were far from a free-flowing outfit, they were skilled at getting the job done.

By contrast France had a team that had grown as the tournament went on and they were looking fast, skilful and potent. They had conceded a goal after just twenty-seven seconds in their opener to England, which ended in a disappointing defeat, but since that setback the French had improved, with the likes of Giresse, Rocheteau, Trésor and the peerless Platini they had players of skill, verve and courage; they would give Germany a game.

Germany started well, wide man Littbarski firing home a rebound from the edge of the penalty area as they finally appeared to be approaching their star billing. When France's Platini cooly equalised from the penalty spot ten minutes later, the semi-final was building up nicely; both teams had remembered to bring their boots with them and it seemed we had a contest to savour.

Just before the hour mark, with France warming to their task, Platini, the visionary, jinked the ball over a static German defence for the onrushing Battiston to attack. Seconds after the Frenchman reached the ball keeper Schumacer clattered into him with the sort of body check Giant Haystacks or Big Daddy would have been proud of. Battiston was left prostrate, with two teeth missing and three cracked ribs, and was not moving. The foul was sickening to witness, yet Schumacer, by now coolly chewing gum waiting for the restart, and was never penalised for probably the notorious foul in World Cup history – no free kick, no penalty, no red card, nothing.

Still shell-shocked by the injuries inflicted on Patrick Battiston, France had to somehow regroup and just keep going; they did and with seconds left of injury time they very nearly won it. Left back Amoros was left unchallenged 30 yards from goal and hit a fierce dipping shot which swerved and dipped past Schumacer's fully outstretched dive only to crash into the crossbar; the French were literally centimetres from the final.

In the first period of extra time the French did more than keep going – they scored two sumptuous goals, first Trésor, a centre back not a centre forward, hooked home from a Giresse free-kick. Five minutes later, Rocheteau, Platini and Six combined to set up Giresse on the edge of the area and he thumped an immaculate shot low to Schumacer's right and in off the post.

Millions of viewers around the world imagined that at 3-1, the Football Gods had finally caught up with West Germany and that the villains of the peace would be exiting, dismantled by the talented French team. Quite rightly, though, the German team had their own ideas, and surrendering to France was not part of the script. Within minutes unfit substitute Karl-Heinz Rummenigge bundled a near post cross past Ettori into the France goal to leave the match fantastically poised. Both sides were now just fifteen minutes from football's biggest occasion and the game was impossible to call. On the one hand France still led, but were clearly tiring; Germany, by contrast, were more experienced at the business end of tournaments – they knew how to just keep winning.

After three minutes of the final period Littbarski crossed from the left to the far post, Rumminegge rose highest and nodded the ball down to the edge of the 6-yard box where Klaus Fischer, falling over and with his back to goal, bicycle-kicked the ball into the top of the French net for a goal of breathtaking execution. Neither team could force the issue in the remaining minutes and for the first time in World Cup history, a penalty shoot-out beckoned.

After such an epic two-hour drama, to calmly pick the ball up, place it on its spot and fire home was no easy task; the players were physically and mentally exhausted, yet eight out of the first ten takers converted. Next up was Maxime Bossis, who watched in agony as Schumacer propelled himself to his right to push the ball out, moments later Hrubesch converted the winning kick to put Germany through. Following his earlier assault on Patrick Battiston, Schumacer was perhaps the most hated hero of any penalty shoot-out there has ever been – not disliked like a pantomine villain, more despised like a serial killer.

Some believe that like one of Shakespeare's tragic heroes France were left bereft and beaten, with no-one to blame but themselves; at 3-1 up in a World Cup semi-final they had had their chance, but simply lost their nerve. A different reading of events points to the unfairness of West Germany's goalkeeper being allowed to play on after an assault that was tantamount

to actual bodily harm. While the views can be debated all
night, what cannot be denied is that this was football of the
very greatest drama imaginable. It simply had the lot: an
iconic occasion, high-class goals, a stirring fightback, unbearable tension and a talking point like no other – the blueprint
for football magic.

THE NUMBERS GAME

These numbers stack up ...

145 was the number of games in which Ian Rush scored for Liverpool and never appeared on the losing side. When Rush put Liverpool ahead in the 1987 League Cup Final against Arsenal, it seemed the cup would surely go back to Merseyside, but, the sequence was finally halted as Arsenal came from behind to win 2-1. The run, which lasted over six years, coincided with some of Liverpool's finest ever seasons; between late 1981 and April 1987, Rush accrued four league championships, three League Cups, one FA Cup success and the 1984 European Cup. Both Rush himself and Liverpool in general had an air of invincibility about them for much of that time. Ironically enough though, the following week lightning appeared to strike for a second time as once again Rush scored only for Liverpool to lose 2-1 to Norwich City – the Midas touch, it seemed, was fading just a little.

14 players was all that was needed for Aston Villa to secure the 1980/81 League Championship in their first title-winning season for seventy-one years. Masterminding Villa's success was manager Ron Saunders, who, long before the days of squad rotation, relied on such consistency of selection that seven players remained ever-present throughout the campaign! Villa's nearest challengers, Ipswich Town, pushed them close, beating Villa in all three meetings, but had to be content with a runners-up slot, an FA Cup semi-final defeat and a UEFA Cup victory.

241 was the number of consecutive matches that Coventry City goalkeeper Steve Ogrizovic played between August 1984 and September 1989, including 209 Division One appearances. Oggy, as he was universally known, was a model of consistently high-quality goalkeeping in an often-struggling Sky Blue outfit. He played on for sixteen seasons at Coventry, until the age of 42, and perhaps not coincidentally in the first season after his retirement Coventry were relegated after thirty-four years in the top flight.

CLOUGH

To be a multiple winner of the League Cup, a League Champion with two different middling-sized clubs a double champion of Europe is an extraordinary feat. To come close to that kind of roll of honour you need a wide and varied skillset: an eye for a bargain, tactical acumen and an unerring ability to lead and inspire. Step forward ... Brian Clough. He had the whole kitbag of managerial tools in his DNA and then a few extra ingredients all of his own, and the results he and Peter Taylor engineered with Nottingham Forest were spectacular.

As the decade opened, Clough was already a European Champion, his Forest team having defeated Sweden's Malmö in the 1979 final. That was a remarkable enough achievement, but in the spring of 1980 Clough's Forest side set about repeating the trick. Wins over Swedish, Romanian, German and Dutch opposition sent Forest to the final in Real Madrid's Santiago Bernabéu Stadium to play Kevin Keegan's Hamburg.

Clough could have opted for any range of pre-match warm ups, repetitive drills, intensive tactical awareness sessions, even poring over detailed dossiers of the opposition. However, Clough eschewed all manner of emerging sports science preparation and simply did things his own way. Before the semi-final against Ajax, he let his team wander through the red-light district in Amsterdam in search of a quiet beer or two. His team talks (preceeded by his preferred music, perhaps Matt Monro or Frank Sinatra) barely lasted a single minute, often consisting of showing his charges a ball and telling them it was their best friend for the next two hours. And prior to the final against Hamburg, keeper Shilton famously trained on a roundabout in the middle of a dual carriageway, as it was one of the few places where there was any decent amount of grass! It was hardly your typical preparation even then – indeed it might have made a Roy-Keane-type perfectionist head home for the nearest airport – but Clough's idiosyncracies had one great thing to commend them: they worked, again and again and again!

In that 1980 final Forest scored an early goal from John Robertson and thereafter refused to give Hamburg, Keegan et al. a sight of their goal. One of the few opportunities Hamburg crafted was a long-range piledriver from full back Manny Kaltz, but Shilton stood firm and simply would not be beaten. Not six months into the new decade, Clough could now place two European Cup winners' medals next to his trademark green jersey; his reputation was sky high and there seemed to be no heights Forest could not scale.

Seen in that light it might be possible to say the rest of the decade became a period of underachievement for Forest: only one more European semi-final, no more league titles and a solitary League Cup win in 1989. That would be a tough assessment of Forest under Clough, though; rather it might be worth looking at things the other way round. For him to have masterminded league and European trophies must have represented a period of astonishing overachievement for a club of Forest's size and potential. Not even Jesus could perform miracles every day!

Statistics will only tell you part of any story, and there are many more parts of the Clough tale that remain pleasingly unquantifiable. For him to take Forest up, turn them into winners and keep them as one of the top flight's most pleasing teams to watch was a massive achievement in its own right. Clough ensured his players move and caress the ball around the pitch, there was to be no route-one hoofing into the channels on his watch. He also insisted on player discipline and discouraged diving or any hectoring of referees;

though he did not always act like a saint himself, he made sure his players were more saintly than diabolical.

Away from his impressive footballing achievements though, it was Clough the character who left such an indelible imprint on both football and the nation. Already a national star from the seventies, when appearances on *Parkinson* showcased his verbal jousting with Muhammad Ali, Clough was one of those people that everyone, even your granny who hated football, knew about. Being regularly mimicked by impressionist Mike Yarwood maintained his sky-high profile, and it never really dipped. Whether in the dugout or the pundit's studio, Clough chastised and charmed in equal measure; never dull and never ignored, he brightened up the football canvas in a way few before or since ever could.

WHAT'S IN A NAME?

Plain, unadorned football shirts replete with modest club badges and Admiral or Umbro logos used to be about all our footballers would wear. Team shirts could stay largely unchanged for, what by today's standards, were unfathomably long periods of time. Only occasional alterations to collars or cuffs would indicate the passing of time; these days glancing through any of the retro shirt catalogues suggests a kind of timeless quality about the old-style strips.

Nothing can stand in the way of progress however, and as the seventies merged into the eighties attitudes, just like fashions, started to change. The once prohibited shirt adverts that were thought to sully the team's jersey, slowly started to become part of the footballer's landscape. As perceptions changed, adverts on shirts came in from the cold, going from a signal of unadulterated greed and a betrayal of the essence of sport to standard issue, a key component in generating income.

The first shirts to host advertising were actually in the 1970s and met with both reluctance and outright resistance. Kettering Town, in a first for the British game, played in shirts emblazoned with 'Kettering Tyres' in January 1976. It had been the idea of ex-Wolves striker and now Kettering CEO, Derek Doogan, who spotted an opening in the commercial world that was ahead of its time. The FA outlawed the move almost immediately, although within a year they were rethinking that policy.

In the professional ranks, Liverpool were first to sign on the dotted line in 1979, with Japanese electronics giant Hitachi. The move was met with much reluctance initially and the Reds were not allowed to wear the sponsor's logo in European or live televised domestic games. At £50,000 a year, though, Liverpool could afford to take the hit to their reputation and pocket the good money. The lukewarm attitude to advertising in other quarters was destined not to last, and by the mid eighties most teams had gone out and got themselves a commercial sponsor to blaze across their newly puffed-out chests.

If there was a debate back then about the increasing commercialisation of the game, or about clubs selling out their heritage and history, it probably didn't last long. Former Arsenal Chairman Peter Hill-Wood might just have been typical when he declared he had initially been against shirt advertising, but had been persuaded of its merits over time – most likely helped by a reputed £500,000 sponsorship deal Arsenal picked up from another Japanese electrical company, JVC. In the days before mind-boggling billion-pound TV deals, clubs simply needed money wherever they could find it, and shirt sponsorship was a pretty straightforward revenue stream to wade into.

The early days of shirt sponsorship did see smaller logos than we get today, and the range of sponsors reflected the more parochial nature of the game three decades ago. Everton were sponsored by Hafnia Ham, a Danish canned meat company, Coventry City by local stationers Tallon Pens, and West Bromwich Albion played with the national 'No Smoking' logos on their shirts – not a multinational, international leading brand in sight.

Leading clubs can now rake in anything up to £40 or £50 million pounds annually from shirt deals with the likes of Chevrolet, or Standard Chartered. Interestingly, the Kettering Tyres deal that began shirt sponsorship allegedly involved a four-figure deal, while the current Chelsea deal with Yokohama Tyres (like Kettering but a more wide-reaching!) is reputedly worth a cool £50 million – the wheel has surely turned!

GREGORY'S GIRL

As a mainstay of British cultural life, football often pops its head into other areas of life, sometimes with great results, sometimes not. So when Bill Forsyth's tale of adolescent love, *Gregory's Girl*, hit the screens back in 1980, based on the premise that love-interest Dorothy was the best footballer in the team, not everyone eagerly awaited its debut. But for once the sceptics were wrong and here was a gem of a film, linked to football, but not led by it.

The film takes a gentle, humorous look at teenage boys and their floundering attempts to impress the opposite sex. The boys here are no Ronaldos. Their personal grooming is not a strength; they spray deodorant on to their shirts and try to impress girls with stats about the velocity of their snot!

The story focuses on Gregory, an awkward teenager who is mad about football and girls, but sadly he's not much good with either. After an eighth successive loss, PE teacher Phil puts the lanky Gregory in goal and, against his better judgement, plays the best player at the trials, Dorothy, up front. She is a revelation, scoring the goal that ends the losing streak, and all the boys want to offer her celebratory kisses. This is almost too much for Gregory who stumbles his way through extra lunchtime practices with her, desperate for a date.

The action scenes are smartly limited to a few keepie-uppies from actress Dee Hepburn and a soft goal or two in 'real-time', which helps to convince the audience that Gregory's team really are rubbish. As the tale progresses Dorothy improbably agrees to date Gregory, before Altered Images pin-up Clare Grogan steals both the show and the man, leaving actor John Gordon Sinclair happier than if he'd scored a winner at Hampden.

The film is cleverly made and even poignant at times as the hapless males are led a merry dance around the football pitch and beyond by streetwise, mature girls who read them like a book and play them like a tune. The football is not overdone, but comes across as credible; it's less Hollywood than the *Goal!* franchise, and more down to earth. Years later, it retains the ability to make you laugh, quite possibly at your younger self!

DEAL OR NO DEAL

In early 1985, when football clubs sought to negotiate a new TV deal for the following seasons, they confidently rejected offers from the BBC and ITV, believing they could get more. The offer of £16 million over four years was more than football had ever received from TV companies before, but for club chairmen it was not enough; they were sure they could do better. Seemingly oblivious to the twin scourges of the national game, declining attendances and increasing stadium disorder, the clubs did not seem to understand that their 'brand' was at best devalued. The negotiations that started in January 1985 continued into February and then May, but failed to produce a positive result. After the disasters at Bradford and Heysel football was toxic in the eyes of many, but club chairmen seemed not to notice.

Back then the TV companies, not the clubs, were all-powerful; they did not need football like football needed them and consequently the TV people were prepared to accept a time when there would be no football on our screens. The idea was basically that 'no deal is better than a bad deal', and while today that is the sort of line favoured by the Prime Minister, years ago it was a simple fact – if you don't like our offer you may as well go and get a referee's whistle ...

Thus for the first half of the 1985/86 season there was a football blackout on the nation's screens and when the impasse was finally broken, (alternatively, when the chairmen came to their senses) the clubs signed up for a deal that was worth less than the original offer. In December 1985, the Football League accepted £1.3 million to show nine First Division and League Cup games before the end of that season. They then signed up for £3.1 million a year, after originally being offered £4 million a year for the following two seasons.

In the current climate of Premier League TV deals raking in over £5 billion between 2016–19, the figures bandied around thirty years ago look like the loose change you find in an old coat pocket. Football had no idea that a huge surge in interest was on the way, and what is commonplace today – the notions of global marketing, subscription sports channels and £10 million matches – could not have been dreamt up by the wildest of *Tomorrow's World* presenters. At the time no one knew football was about to become awash with mega-shops, mega-stars and mega-salaries; the keys in the ignition of the commercial juggernaut were just about to turn.

MOMENT IN TIME:
MICHAEL THOMAS, 1989

When Liverpool and Arsenal lined up against each other at Anfield, in May 1989, football was very much under the shadow of the Hillsborough tragedy, which had occurred just six weeks earlier. The opportunity to focus on events on the pitch for a brief time could not begin to assuage the rawest of grief, but the title-decider was a welcome diversion. The match itself was the first time for almost forty years that two teams had met in the final game with both still having a chance of being champions; the once-in-a-generation (or two) occasion did not disappoint.

In the red corner were Dalglish's all-conquering Liverpool team, fresh from winning the FA Cup, and looking to secure yet another championship. In the yellow and blue corner were George Graham's superbly drilled Arsenal, without a title for eighteen years but very much a team in the ascendancy; the division's top scorers had led for much of the season. However, after gathering just one point from their final two home matches, Arsenal were conspiring to finish second in what had seemed at one time a one-horse ace. Liverpool's tremendous run of fifteen wins and three draws in eighteen games seemed as perfectly timed as most of their passing movements and the title looked Anfield-bound.

On the night the odds massively favoured Liverpool; they could afford to draw or even lose by a single goal and the championship would still be theirs. Arsenal needed something special, almost miraculous. What they did have was a canny manager in George Graham, and he had a plan. Arsenal switched to a back five for the night, with Graham reasoning that the longer the game was goalless, the better the chance for his men to nick something. In a cagey first half, Arsenal played a good containing game; not much came John Lukic's way in goal and the Liverpool spearhead of Barnes, Aldridge and Rush was blunted.

When Alan Smith glanced home a Nigel Winterburn free kick seven minutes after the interval the complexion of the match changed; now ahead on the night and with nearly forty minutes to score again, Arsenal had firmly planted doubts into Liverpool's minds. As Anfield crackled with tension, Arsenal became more assured and attack-minded while Liverpool nerves frayed. Fifteen minutes from time Michael Thomas received the ball in space near the Liverpool penalty spot, but prodded the ball within Grobbelaar's reach; with that save it seemed likely that Arsenal's best chance might have gone.

In memorable images, ITV cameras then captured Liverpool's Steve McMahon exhorting his teammates, with index finger raised, to indicate they were just one minute from the championship. Liverpool were desperately close; close enough to probably smell the polish on the trophy, but not close enough for John Barnes to take the ball to the corner flag. Instead Barnes, a forward of rare pace, power and skill, decided to attempt another dribble, this time deep into the Arsenal penalty area, only to be dispossessed by Kevin Richardson, allowing Arsenal the chance to start one final attack.

To Arsenal fans what followed will, like an actor's well-rehearsed lines, be with them forever: Lukic's throw, Dixon's long ball, Smith's through ball and then Michael Thomas bursting into the penalty area. Just seconds after Barnes lost possession in front of the Kop, Arsenal fans were about to lose their minds as Michael Thomas nudged the ball into Grobbelaar's net for the championship winner.

Although Italia '90 is often cited as the moment in which football started to finally drag itself from the doldrums, arguably the green shoots of recovery can be traced to that title showdown at Anfield. The match was rare for both the highest of stakes it represented and for the fact that it was one the few games broadcast on live national TV at the time. As 8 million viewers tuned in to endure and enjoy the unfolding drama, TV executives saw the potential of live coverage and with satellite technology imminent, a new era of televised football.

LEAGUE RESULTS

Italics denote teams promoted or relegated in each season

1979/80

League Division 1

		P	W	D	L	F	A	W	D	L	F	A	Pts
1	Liverpool	42	15	6	0	46	8	10	4	7	35	22	60
2	Manchester United	42	17	3	1	43	8	7	7	7	22	27	58
3	Ipswich Town	42	14	4	3	43	13	8	5	8	25	26	53
4	Arsenal	42	8	10	3	24	12	10	6	5	28	24	52
5	Nottingham Forest	42	16	4	1	44	11	4	4	13	19	32	48
6	Wolverhampton Wanderers	42	9	6	6	29	20	10	3	8	29	27	47
7	Aston Villa	42	11	5	5	29	22	5	9	7	22	28	46
8	Southampton	42	14	2	5	53	24	4	7	10	12	29	45
9	Middlesbrough	42	11	7	3	31	14	5	5	11	19	30	44
10	West Bromwich Albion	42	9	8	4	37	23	2	11	8	17	27	41
11	Leeds United	42	10	7	4	30	17	3	7	11	16	33	40
12	Norwich City	42	10	8	3	38	30	3	6	12	20	36	40
13	Crystal Palace	42	9	9	3	26	13	3	7	11	15	37	40

		P	W	D	L	F	A	W	D	L	F	A	Pts
14	Tottenham Hotspur	42	11	5	5	30	22	4	5	12	22	40	40
15	Coventry City	42	12	2	7	34	24	4	5	12	22	42	39
16	Brighton & Hove Albion	42	8	8	5	25	20	3	7	11	22	37	37
17	Manchester City	42	8	8	5	28	25	4	5	12	15	41	37
18	Stoke City	42	9	4	8	27	26	4	6	11	17	32	36
19	Everton	42	7	7	7	28	25	2	10	9	15	26	35
20	Bristol City	42	6	6	9	22	30	3	7	11	15	36	31
21	Derby County	42	9	4	8	36	29	2	4	15	11	38	30
22	Bolton Wanderers	42	5	11	5	19	21	0	4	17	19	52	25

League Division 2

		P	W	D	L	F	A	W	D	L	F	A	Pts
1	Leicester City	42	12	5	4	32	19	9	8	4	26	19	55
2	Sunderland	42	16	5	0	47	13	5	7	9	22	29	54
3	Birmingham City	42	14	5	2	37	16	7	6	8	21	22	53
4	Chelsea	42	14	3	4	34	16	9	4	8	32	36	53
5	Queen's Park Rangers	42	10	9	2	46	25	8	4	9	29	28	49
6	Luton Town	42	9	10	2	36	17	7	7	7	30	28	49
7	West Ham United	42	13	2	6	37	21	7	5	9	17	22	47
8	Cambridge United	42	11	6	4	40	23	3	10	8	21	30	44
9	Newcastle United	42	13	6	2	35	19	2	8	11	18	30	44
10	Preston North End	42	8	10	3	30	23	4	9	8	26	29	43

11	Oldham Athletic	42	12	5	4	30	21	4	6	11	19	32	43
12	Swansea City	42	13	1	7	31	20	4	8	9	17	33	43
13	Shrewsbury Town	42	12	3	6	41	23	6	2	13	19	30	41
14	Leyton Orient	42	7	9	5	29	31	5	8	8	19	23	41
15	Cardiff City	42	11	4	6	21	16	5	4	12	20	32	40
16	Wrexham	42	13	2	6	26	15	3	4	14	14	34	38
17	Notts County	42	4	11	6	24	22	7	4	10	27	30	37
18	Watford	42	9	6	6	27	18	3	7	11	12	28	37
19	Bristol Rovers	42	9	8	4	33	23	2	5	14	17	41	35
20	Fulham	42	6	4	11	19	28	5	3	13	23	46	29
21	Burnley	42	5	9	7	19	23	1	6	14	20	50	27
22	Charlton Athletic	42	6	6	9	25	31	0	4	17	14	47	22

League Division 3

		P	W	D	L	F	A	W	D	L	F	A	Pts
1	Grimsby Town	46	18	2	3	46	16	8	8	7	27	26	62
2	Blackburn Rovers	46	13	5	5	34	17	12	4	7	24	19	59
3	Sheffield Wednesday	46	12	6	5	44	20	9	10	4	37	27	58
4	Chesterfield	46	16	5	2	46	16	7	6	10	25	30	57
5	Colchester United	46	10	10	3	39	20	10	2	11	25	36	52
6	Carlisle United	46	13	6	4	45	26	5	6	12	21	30	48
7	Reading	46	14	6	3	43	19	2	10	11	23	46	48

		P	W	D	L	F	A	W	D	L	F	A		Pts
8	Exeter City	46	14	5	4	38	22	5	5	13	22	46		48
9	Chester City	46	14	6	3	29	18	3	7	13	20	39		47
10	Swindon Town	46	15	4	4	50	20	4	4	15	21	43		46
11	Barnsley	46	10	7	6	29	20	6	7	10	24	36		46
12	Sheffield United	46	13	5	5	34	21	5	5	13	25	45		46
13	Rotherham United	46	13	4	6	38	24	5	6	12	20	42		46
14	Millwall	46	14	6	3	49	23	2	7	14	16	36		45
15	Plymouth Argyle	46	13	7	3	39	17	3	5	15	20	38		44
16	Gillingham	46	8	9	6	26	18	6	5	12	23	33		42
17	Oxford United	46	10	4	9	34	24	4	9	10	23	38		41
18	Blackpool	46	10	7	6	39	34	5	4	14	23	40		41
19	Brentford	46	10	6	7	33	26	5	5	13	26	47		41
20	Hull City	46	11	7	5	29	21	1	9	13	22	48		40
21	Bury	46	10	7	9	30	23	6	3	14	15	36		39
22	Southend United	46	11	6	6	33	23	3	4	16	14	34		38
23	Mansfield Town	46	9	9	5	31	24	1	7	15	16	34		36
24	Wimbledon	46	6	8	9	34	38	4	6	13	18	43		34

League Division 4

		P	W	D	L	F	A	W	D	L	F	A	Pts
1	Huddersfield Town	46	16	5	2	61	18	11	7	5	40	30	66
2	Walsall	46	12	9	2	43	23	11	9	3	32	24	64

Pos	Team	P	W	D	L	F	A	W	D	L	F	A	Pts
3	*Newport County*	46	16	5	2	47	22	11	2	10	36	28	61
4	*Portsmouth*	46	15	5	3	62	23	9	7	7	29	26	60
5	Bradford City	46	14	6	3	44	14	10	6	7	33	36	60
6	Wigan Athletic	46	13	5	5	42	26	8	8	7	34	35	55
7	Lincoln City	46	14	8	1	43	12	4	9	10	21	30	53
8	Peterborough United	46	14	3	6	39	22	7	7	9	19	25	52
9	Torquay United	46	13	7	3	47	25	2	10	11	23	44	47
10	Aldershot	46	10	7	6	35	23	6	6	11	27	30	45
11	Bournemouth	46	8	9	6	32	25	5	9	9	20	26	44
12	Doncaster Rovers	46	11	6	6	37	27	4	8	11	25	36	44
13	Northampton	46	14	5	4	33	16	2	7	14	18	50	44
14	Scunthorpe United	46	11	9	3	37	23	3	6	14	21	52	43
15	Tranmere Rovers	46	10	4	9	32	24	4	9	10	18	32	41
16	Stockport County	46	9	7	7	30	31	5	5	13	18	41	40
17	York City	46	9	6	8	35	34	5	5	13	30	48	39
18	Halifax Town	46	11	9	3	29	20	2	5	17	17	52	39
19	Hartlepool United	46	10	7	6	36	28	4	3	16	23	36	38
20	Port Vale	46	8	6	9	34	24	4	6	13	22	46	36
21	Hereford United	46	8	7	8	22	21	3	7	13	16	31	36
22	Darlington	46	7	11	5	33	26	2	6	15	17	48	35
23	Crewe Alexandra	46	10	6	7	25	27	1	7	15	10	41	35
24	Rochdale	46	6	7	10	20	28	1	6	16	13	51	27

Season 1980-81

League Division 1

		P	W	D	L	F	A	W	D	L	F	A	Pts
1	Aston Villa	42	16	3	2	40	13	10	5	6	32	27	60
2	Ipswich Town	42	15	4	2	45	14	8	6	7	32	29	56
3	Arsenal	42	13	8	0	36	17	6	7	8	25	28	53
4	West Bromwich Albion	42	15	4	2	40	15	5	8	8	20	27	52
5	Liverpool	42	13	5	3	38	15	4	12	5	24	27	51
6	Southampton	42	15	4	2	47	22	5	6	10	29	34	50
7	Nottingham Forest	42	15	3	3	44	20	4	9	8	18	24	50
8	Manchester United	42	9	11	1	30	14	6	7	8	21	22	48
9	Leeds United	42	10	5	6	19	19	7	5	9	20	28	44
10	Tottenham Hotspur	42	9	9	3	44	31	5	6	10	26	37	43
11	Stoke City	42	8	9	4	31	23	4	9	8	20	37	42
12.	Manchester City	42	10	7	4	35	25	4	4	13	21	34	39
13	Birmingham City	42	11	5	5	32	23	2	7	12	18	38	38
14	Middlesbrough	42	14	4	3	38	16	2	1	18	15	45	37
15	Everton	42	8	6	7	32	25	5	4	12	23	33	36
16	Coventry City	42	9	6	6	31	30	4	4	13	17	38	36
17	Sunderland	42	10	4	7	32	19	4	3	14	20	34	35
18	Wolverhampton Wanderers	42	11	2	8	26	20	2	7	12	17	35	35

19	Brighton & Hove Albion	42	10	3	8	30	26	4	4	13	24	41	35
20	Norwich City	42	9	7	5	34	25	4	0	17	15	48	33
21	Leicester City	42	7	5	9	20	23	6	1	14	20	44	32
22	Crystal Palace	42	6	4	11	32	37	0	3	18	15	46	19

League Division 2

		P	W	D	L	F	A	W	D	L	F	A	Pts
1	West Ham United	42	19	1	1	53	12	9	9	3	26	17	66
2	Notts County	42	10	8	3	26	15	8	9	4	23	23	53
3	Swansea City	42	12	5	4	39	19	6	9	6	25	25	50
4	Blackburn Rovers	42	12	8	1	28	7	4	10	7	14	22	50
5	Luton Town	42	10	6	5	35	23	8	6	7	26	23	48
6	Derby County	42	9	8	4	34	26	6	7	8	23	26	45
7	Grimsby Town	42	10	8	3	21	10	5	7	9	23	32	45
8	Queen's Park Rangers	42	11	7	3	36	12	4	6	11	20	34	43
9	Watford	42	13	5	3	34	18	3	6	12	16	27	43
10	Sheffield Wednesday	42	14	4	3	38	14	3	4	14	15	37	42
11	Newcastle United	42	11	7	3	22	13	3	7	11	8	32	42
12	Chelsea	42	8	6	7	27	15	6	6	9	19	26	40
13	Cambridge United	42	13	1	7	36	23	4	5	12	17	42	40
14	Shrewsbury Town	42	9	7	5	33	22	2	10	9	13	25	39
15	Oldham Athletic	42	7	9	5	19	16	5	6	10	20	32	39

16	Wrexham	42	5	8	8	22	24	7	6	8	21	21	38
17	Leyton Orient	42	9	8	4	34	20	4	4	13	18	36	38
18	Bolton Wanderers	42	10	5	6	40	27	4	5	12	21	39	38
19	Cardiff City	42	7	7	7	23	24	5	5	11	21	36	36
20	Preston North End	42	8	7	6	28	26	3	7	11	13	36	36
21	Bristol City	42	6	10	5	19	15	1	6	14	10	36	30
22	Bristol Rovers	42	4	9	8	21	24	1	4	16	13	41	23

League Division 3

		P	W	D	L	F	A	W	D	L	F	A	Pts
1	Rotherham United	46	17	6	0	43	8	7	7	9	19	24	61
2	Barnsley	46	15	5	3	46	19	6	12	5	26	26	59
3	Charlton Athletic	46	14	6	3	36	17	11	3	9	27	27	59
4	Huddersfield Town	46	14	6	3	40	11	7	8	8	31	29	56
5	Chesterfield	46	17	4	2	42	16	6	6	11	30	32	56
6	Portsmouth	46	14	5	4	35	19	8	4	11	20	28	53
7	Plymouth Argyle	46	14	5	4	35	18	5	9	9	21	26	52
8	Burnley	46	13	5	5	37	21	5	9	9	23	27	50
9	Brentford	46	7	9	7	30	25	7	10	6	22	24	47
10	Reading	46	13	5	5	39	22	5	5	13	23	40	46
11	Exeter City	46	9	9	5	36	30	7	4	12	26	36	45
12	Newport County	46	11	6	6	38	22	4	7	12	26	39	43

		P	W	D	L	F	A	W	D	L	F	A	Pts
13	Fulham	46	8	7	8	28	29	7	6	10	29	35	43
14	Oxford United	46	7	8	8	20	24	6	9	8	19	23	43
15	Gillingham	46	9	8	6	23	19	3	10	10	25	39	42
16	Millwall	46	10	9	4	30	21	4	5	14	13	39	42
17	Swindon Town	46	10	6	7	35	27	3	9	11	16	29	41
18	Chester City	46	11	5	7	25	17	4	6	13	13	31	41
19	Carlisle United	46	8	9	6	32	29	6	4	13	24	41	41
20	Walsall	46	8	9	6	43	43	5	6	12	16	31	41
21	Sheffield United	46	12	6	5	38	20	2	6	15	27	43	40
22	Colchester United	46	12	7	4	35	22	2	4	17	10	43	39
23	Blackpool	46	5	9	9	19	28	4	5	14	26	47	32
24	Hull City	46	7	8	8	23	22	1	8	14	17	49	32

League Division 4

		P	W	D	L	F	A	W	D	L	F	A	Pts
1	Southend United	46	19	4	0	47	6	11	3	9	32	25	67
2	Lincoln City	46	15	7	1	44	11	10	8	5	22	14	65
3	Doncaster Rovers	46	15	4	4	36	20	7	8	8	23	29	56
4	Wimbledon	46	15	4	4	42	17	8	5	10	22	29	55
5	Peterborough United	46	11	8	4	37	21	6	10	7	31	33	52
6	Aldershot	46	12	9	2	28	11	6	5	12	15	30	50
7	Mansfield Town	46	13	5	5	36	15	7	4	12	22	29	49

		P	W	D	L	F	A	W	D	L	F	A	Pts
8	Darlington	46	13	6	4	43	23	6	5	12	22	36	49
9	Hartlepool United	46	14	3	6	42	22	6	6	11	22	39	49
10	Northampton	46	11	7	5	42	26	7	6	10	23	41	49
11	Wigan Athletic	46	13	4	6	29	16	5	7	11	22	39	47
12	Bury	46	10	8	5	38	21	7	3	13	32	41	45
13	Bournemouth	46	9	8	6	30	21	7	5	11	17	27	45
14	Bradford City	46	9	9	5	30	24	5	7	11	23	36	44
15	Rochdale	46	11	6	6	33	25	3	9	11	27	45	43
16	Scunthorpe United	46	8	12	3	40	31	3	8	12	20	38	42
17	Torquay United	46	13	2	8	38	26	5	3	15	17	37	41
18	Crewe Alexandra	46	10	7	6	28	20	3	7	13	20	41	40
19	Port Vale	46	10	8	5	40	23	2	7	14	17	47	39
20	Stockport County	46	10	5	8	29	25	6	2	15	15	32	39
21	Tranmere Rovers	46	12	5	6	41	24	1	5	17	18	49	36
22	Hereford United	46	8	8	7	29	20	3	5	15	9	42	35
23	Halifax Town	46	9	3	11	28	32	2	9	12	16	39	34
24	York City	46	10	2	11	31	23	2	7	14	16	43	33

Season 1981/82

League Division 1

		P	W	D	L	F	A	W	D	L	F	A	Pts
1	Liverpool	42	14	3	4	39	14	12	6	3	41	18	87
2	Ipswich Town	42	17	1	3	47	25	9	4	8	28	28	83
3	Manchester United	42	12	6	3	27	9	10	6	5	32	20	78
4	Tottenham Hotspur	42	12	4	5	41	26	8	7	6	26	22	71
5	Arsenal	42	13	5	3	27	15	7	6	8	21	22	71
6	Swansea City	42	13	3	5	34	16	8	3	10	24	35	69
7	Southampton	42	15	2	4	49	30	4	7	10	23	37	66
8	Everton	42	11	7	3	33	21	6	6	9	23	29	64
9	West Ham United	42	9	10	2	42	29	5	6	10	24	28	58
10	Manchester City	42	9	7	5	32	23	6	6	9	17	27	58
11	Aston Villa	42	9	6	6	28	24	6	6	9	27	29	57
12	Nottingham Forest	42	7	7	7	19	20	8	5	8	23	28	57
13	Brighton & Hove Albion	42	8	7	6	30	24	5	6	10	13	28	52
14	Coventry City	42	9	4	8	31	24	4	7	10	25	38	50
15	Notts County	42	8	5	8	32	33	5	3	13	29	36	47
16	Birmingham City	42	8	6	7	29	25	2	8	11	24	36	44
17	West Bromwich Albion	42	6	6	9	24	25	5	5	11	22	32	44
18	Stoke City	42	9	2	10	27	28	3	6	12	17	35	44

19	Sunderland	42	6	5	10	19	26	5	6	10	19	32	44
20	*Leeds United*	42	6	11	4	23	20	4	1	16	16	41	42
21	*Wolverhampton Wanderers*	42	8	5	8	19	20	2	5	14	13	43	40
22	*Middlesbrough*	42	5	9	7	20	24	3	6	12	14	28	39

League Division 2

		P	W	D	L	F	A	W	D	L	F	A	Pts
1	*Luton Town*	42	16	3	2	48	19	9	10	2	38	27	88
2	*Watford*	42	13	6	2	46	16	10	5	6	30	26	80
3	*Norwich City*	42	14	3	4	41	19	8	2	11	23	31	71
4	Sheffield Wednesday	42	10	8	3	31	23	10	2	9	24	28	70
5	Queen's Park Rangers	42	15	4	2	40	9	6	2	13	25	34	69
6	Barnsley	42	13	4	4	33	14	6	6	9	26	27	67
7	Rotherham United	42	13	5	3	42	19	7	2	12	24	35	67
8	Leicester City	42	12	5	4	31	19	6	7	8	25	29	66
9	Newcastle United	42	14	4	3	30	14	4	4	13	22	36	62
10	Blackburn Rovers	42	11	4	6	26	15	5	7	9	21	28	59
11	Oldham Athletic	42	9	9	3	28	23	6	5	10	22	28	59
12	Chelsea	42	10	5	6	37	30	5	7	9	23	30	57
13	Charlton Athletic	42	11	5	5	33	22	2	7	12	17	43	51
14	Cambridge United	42	11	4	6	31	19	2	5	14	17	34	48

		P	W	D	L	F	A	W	D	L	F	A	Pts
15	Crystal Palace	42	9	2	10	25	26	4	7	10	9	19	48
16	Derby County	42	9	8	4	32	23	3	4	14	21	45	48
17	Grimsby Town	42	5	8	8	29	30	6	5	10	24	35	46
18	Shrewsbury Town	42	10	6	5	26	19	1	7	13	11	38	46
19	Bolton Wanderers	42	10	4	7	28	24	3	3	15	11	37	46
20	Cardiff City	42	9	2	10	28	32	3	6	12	17	29	44
21	Wrexham	42	9	4	8	22	22	2	7	12	18	34	44
22	Leyton Orient	42	6	8	7	23	24	4	1	16	13	37	39

League Division 3

		P	W	D	L	F	A	W	D	L	F	A	Pts
1	Burnley	46	13	7	3	37	20	8	10	5	29	25	80
2	Carlisle United	46	17	4	2	44	21	6	7	10	21	29	80
3	Fulham	46	12	9	2	44	22	9	6	8	33	29	78
4	Lincoln City	46	13	7	3	40	16	8	7	8	26	24	77
5	Oxford United	46	10	8	5	28	18	8	6	8	35	31	71
6	Gillingham	46	14	5	4	44	26	6	6	11	20	30	71
7	Southend United	46	11	7	5	35	23	7	6	8	28	28	69
8	Brentford	46	8	6	9	28	22	11	5	7	28	25	68
9	Millwall	46	12	4	7	36	28	6	9	8	26	34	67
10	Plymouth Argyle	46	12	5	6	37	24	6	6	11	27	32	65

		P	W	D	L	F	A	W	D	L	F	A	Pts
11	Chesterfield	46	12	4	7	33	27	6	6	11	24	31	64
12	Reading	46	11	6	6	43	35	6	5	12	24	40	62
13	Portsmouth	46	11	10	2	33	14	3	9	11	23	37	61
14	Preston North End	46	10	7	6	25	22	6	6	11	25	34	61
15	Bristol Rovers	46	12	4	7	35	28	6	5	12	23	37	61
16	Newport County	46	9	10	4	28	21	5	6	12	26	33	58
17	Huddersfield Town	46	10	5	8	38	25	5	7	11	26	34	57
18	Exeter City	46	14	4	5	46	34	2	5	16	25	51	57
19	Doncaster Rovers	46	9	9	5	31	24	4	8	11	24	44	56
20	Walsall	46	10	7	6	32	23	3	7	13	19	32	53
21	Wimbledon	46	10	6	7	33	27	4	5	14	28	48	53
22	Swindon Town	46	9	5	9	37	36	4	8	11	18	35	52
23	Bristol City	46	7	6	10	24	29	4	7	12	17	36	46
24	Chester City	46	2	10	11	16	30	5	1	17	20	48	32

League Division 4

		P	W	D	L	F	A	W	D	L	F	A	Pts
1	Sheffield United	46	15	8	0	53	15	12	7	4	41	26	96
2	Bradford City	46	14	7	2	52	23	12	6	5	36	22	91
3	Wigan Athletic	46	17	5	1	47	18	9	8	6	33	28	91
4	Bournemouth	46	12	10	1	37	15	11	9	3	25	15	88
5	Peterborough United	46	16	3	4	46	22	8	7	8	25	35	82

		P	W	D	L	F	A	W	D	L	F	A	Pts
6	Colchester United	46	12	6	5	47	23	8	6	9	35	34	72
7	Port Vale	46	9	12	2	26	17	9	4	10	30	32	70
8	Hull City	46	14	3	6	36	23	5	9	9	34	38	69
9	Bury	46	13	7	3	53	26	4	10	9	27	33	68
10	Hereford United	46	10	9	4	36	25	6	10	7	28	33	67
11	Tranmere Rovers	46	7	9	7	27	25	7	9	7	24	31	60
12	Blackpool	46	11	5	7	40	26	4	8	11	26	34	58
13	Darlington	46	10	5	8	36	28	5	8	10	25	34	58
14	Hartlepool United	46	9	8	6	39	34	4	8	11	34	50	55
15	Torquay United	46	9	8	6	30	25	5	5	13	17	34	55
16	Aldershot	46	8	7	8	34	29	5	8	10	23	39	54
17	York City	46	9	5	9	45	37	5	3	15	24	54	50
18	Stockport County	46	10	5	8	34	28	2	8	13	14	39	49
19	Halifax Town	46	6	11	6	28	30	3	11	9	23	42	49
20	Mansfield Town	46	7	7	9	39	39	5	4	14	24	42	47
21	Rochdale	46	7	9	7	26	22	3	7	13	24	40	46
22	Northampton	46	9	5	9	32	27	2	4	17	25	57	42
23	Scunthorpe United	46	7	9	7	26	35	2	6	15	17	44	42
24	Crewe Alexandra	46	3	6	14	19	32	3	3	17	10	52	27

Season 1982/83

League Division 1

		P	W	D	L	F	A	W	D	L	F	A	Pts
1	Liverpool	42	16	4	1	55	16	8	6	7	32	21	82
2	Watford	42	16	2	3	49	20	6	3	12	25	37	71
3	Manchester United	42	14	7	0	39	10	5	6	10	17	28	70
4	Tottenham Hotspur	42	15	4	2	50	15	5	5	11	15	35	69
5	Nottingham Forest	42	12	5	4	34	18	8	4	9	28	32	69
6	Aston Villa	42	17	2	2	47	15	4	3	14	15	35	68
7	Everton	42	13	6	2	43	19	5	4	12	23	29	64
8	West Ham United	42	13	3	5	41	23	7	1	13	27	39	64
9	Ipswich Town	42	11	3	7	39	23	4	10	7	25	27	58
10	Arsenal	42	11	6	4	36	19	5	4	12	22	37	58
11	West Bromwich Albion	42	11	5	5	35	20	4	7	10	16	29	57
12	Southampton	42	11	5	5	36	22	4	7	10	18	36	57
13	Stoke City	42	13	4	4	34	21	3	5	13	19	43	57
14	Norwich City	42	10	6	5	30	18	4	6	11	22	40	54
15	Notts County	42	12	4	5	37	25	3	3	15	18	46	52
16	Sunderland	42	7	10	4	30	22	5	4	12	18	39	50
17	Birmingham City	42	9	7	5	29	24	3	7	11	11	31	50
18	Luton Town	42	7	7	7	34	33	5	6	10	31	51	49

		P	W	D	L	F	A	W	D	L	F	A	Pts
19	Coventry City	42	10	5	6	29	17	3	4	14	19	42	48
20	Manchester City	42	9	5	7	26	23	4	3	14	21	47	47
21	Swansea City	42	10	4	7	32	29	0	7	14	19	40	41
22	Brighton & Hove Albion	42	8	7	6	25	22	1	6	14	13	46	40

League Division 2

		P	W	D	L	F	A	W	D	L	F	A	Pts
1	Queens Park Rangers	42	16	3	2	51	16	10	4	7	26	20	85
2	Wolverhampton Wanderers	42	14	5	2	42	16	6	10	5	26	28	75
3	Leicester City	42	11	4	6	36	15	9	6	6	36	29	70
4	Fulham	42	13	5	3	36	20	7	4	10	28	27	69
5	Newcastle United	42	13	6	2	43	21	5	7	9	32	32	67
6	Sheffield Wednesday	42	9	8	4	33	23	7	7	7	27	24	63
7	Oldham Athletic	42	8	10	3	38	24	6	9	6	26	23	61
8	Leeds United	42	7	11	3	28	22	6	10	5	23	24	60
9	Shrewsbury Town	42	8	9	4	20	15	7	5	9	28	33	59
10	Barnsley	42	9	8	4	37	28	5	7	9	20	27	57
11	Blackburn Rovers	42	11	7	3	38	21	4	5	12	20	37	57
12	Cambridge United	42	11	7	3	26	17	2	5	14	16	43	51
13	Derby County	42	7	10	4	27	24	3	9	9	22	34	49
14	Carlisle United	42	10	6	5	44	28	2	6	13	24	42	48
15	Crystal Palace	42	11	7	3	31	17	1	5	15	12	35	48

16	Middlesbrough	42	8	7	6	27	29	3	8	10	19	38	48
17	Charlton Athletic	42	11	3	7	40	31	2	6	13	23	55	48
18	Chelsea	42	8	8	5	31	22	3	6	12	20	39	47
19	Grimsby Town	42	9	7	5	32	26	3	4	14	13	44	47
20	Rotherham United	42	6	7	8	22	29	4	8	9	23	39	45
21	Burnley	42	10	4	7	38	24	2	4	15	18	42	44
22	Bolton Wanderers	42	10	2	9	30	26	1	9	11	12	35	44

League Division 3

		P	W	D	L	F	A	W	D	L	F	A	Pts
1	Portsmouth	46	16	4	3	43	19	11	6	6	31	22	91
2	Cardiff City	46	17	5	1	45	14	8	6	9	31	36	86
3	Huddersfield Town	46	15	8	0	56	18	8	5	10	28	31	82
4	Newport County	46	13	7	3	40	20	10	2	11	36	34	78
5	Oxford United	46	12	9	2	41	23	10	3	10	30	30	78
6	Lincoln City	46	17	1	5	55	22	6	6	11	22	29	76
7	Bristol Rovers	46	16	4	3	55	21	6	5	12	29	37	75
8	Plymouth Argyle	46	15	2	6	37	23	4	6	13	24	43	65
9	Brentford	46	14	4	5	50	28	4	6	13	38	49	64
10	Walsall	46	14	5	4	38	19	3	8	12	26	44	64
11	Sheffield United	46	16	3	4	44	20	3	4	16	18	44	64

		P	W	D	L	F	A	W	D	L	F	A	Pts
12	Bradford City	46	11	7	5	41	27	5	6	12	27	42	61
13	Gillingham	46	12	4	7	37	29	4	9	10	21	30	61
14	Bournemouth	46	11	7	5	35	20	5	6	12	24	48	61
15	Southend United	46	10	8	5	41	28	5	6	12	25	37	59
16	Preston North End	46	11	10	2	35	17	4	3	16	25	52	58
17	Millwall	46	12	7	4	41	24	2	6	15	23	53	55
18	Wigan Athletic	46	10	4	9	35	33	5	5	13	25	39	54
19	Exeter City	46	12	4	7	49	43	2	8	13	32	61	54
20	Leyton Orient	46	10	6	7	44	38	5	3	15	20	50	54
21	Reading	46	10	8	5	37	28	2	9	12	27	51	53
22	Wrexham	46	11	6	6	40	26	1	9	13	16	50	51
23	Doncaster Rovers	46	6	8	9	38	44	3	3	17	19	53	38
24	Chesterfield	46	6	6	11	28	28	2	7	14	15	40	37

League Division 4

		P	W	D	L	F	A	W	D	L	F	A	Pts
1	Wimbledon	46	17	4	2	57	23	12	7	4	39	22	98
2	Hull City	46	14	8	1	48	14	11	7	5	27	20	90
3	Port Vale	46	15	4	4	37	16	11	6	6	30	18	88
4	Scunthorpe United	46	13	7	3	41	17	10	7	6	30	25	83
5	Bury	46	15	4	4	43	20	8	8	7	31	26	81

	Team	P	W	D	L	F	A	W	D	L	F	A	Pts
6	Colchester United	46	17	5	1	51	19	7	4	12	24	36	81
7	York City	46	18	4	1	59	19	4	9	10	29	39	79
8	Swindon Town	46	14	3	6	45	27	5	8	10	16	27	68
9	Peterborough United	46	13	6	4	38	23	4	7	12	20	29	64
10	Mansfield Town	46	11	6	6	32	26	5	7	11	29	44	61
11	Halifax Town	46	9	8	6	31	23	7	4	12	28	43	60
12	Torquay United	46	12	3	8	38	30	5	4	14	18	35	58
13	Chester City	46	8	6	9	28	24	7	5	11	27	36	56
14	Bristol City	46	10	8	5	32	25	3	9	11	27	45	56
15	Northampton	46	10	8	5	43	29	4	4	15	22	46	54
16	Stockport County	46	11	8	4	41	31	3	4	16	19	48	54
17	Darlington	46	8	5	10	27	30	5	8	10	34	41	52
18	Aldershot	46	11	5	7	40	35	1	10	12	21	47	51
19	Tranmere Rovers	46	8	8	7	30	29	5	3	15	19	42	50
20	Rochdale	46	11	8	4	38	25	0	8	15	17	48	49
21	Blackpool	46	10	8	5	32	23	3	4	16	23	51	49
22	Hartlepool United	46	11	5	7	30	24	2	4	17	16	52	48
23	Crewe Alexandra	46	9	5	9	35	32	2	3	18	18	39	41
24	Hereford United	46	8	6	9	19	23	3	2	18	23	56	41

Season 1983/84

Canon League Division 1

		P	W	D	L	F	A	W	D	L	F	A	Pts
1	Liverpool	42	14	5	2	50	12	8	9	4	23	20	80
2	Southampton	42	15	4	2	44	17	7	7	7	22	21	77
3	Nottingham Forest	42	14	4	3	47	17	8	4	9	29	28	74
4	Manchester United	42	14	3	4	43	18	6	11	4	28	23	74
5	Queen's Park Rangers	42	14	4	3	37	12	8	3	10	30	25	73
6	Arsenal	42	10	5	6	41	29	8	4	9	33	31	63
7	Everton	42	9	9	3	21	12	7	5	9	23	30	62
8	Tottenham Hotspur	42	11	4	6	31	24	6	6	9	33	41	61
9	West Ham United	42	10	4	7	39	24	7	5	9	21	31	60
10	Aston Villa	42	14	3	4	34	22	3	6	12	25	39	60
11	Watford	42	9	7	5	36	31	7	2	12	32	46	57
12	Ipswich Town	42	11	4	6	34	23	4	4	13	21	34	53
13	Sunderland	42	8	9	4	26	18	5	4	12	16	35	52
14	Norwich City	42	9	8	4	34	20	3	7	11	14	29	51
15	Leicester City	42	11	5	5	40	30	2	7	12	25	38	51
16	Luton Town	42	7	5	9	30	33	7	4	10	23	33	51
17	West Bromwich Albion	42	10	4	7	30	25	4	5	12	18	37	51
18	Stoke City	42	11	4	6	30	23	2	7	12	14	40	50

		P	W	D	L	F	A	W	D	L	F	A	Pts
19	Coventry City	42	8	5	8	33	33	5	6	10	24	44	50
20	Birmingham City	42	7	7	7	19	18	5	5	11	20	32	48
21	Notts County	42	6	7	8	31	36	4	4	13	19	36	41
22	Wolverhampton Wanderers	42	4	8	9	15	28	2	3	16	12	52	29

Canon League Division 2

		P	W	D	L	F	A	W	D	L	F	A	Pts
1	Chelsea	42	15	4	2	55	17	10	9	2	35	23	88
2	Sheffield Wednesday	42	16	4	1	47	16	10	6	5	25	18	88
3	Newcastle United	42	16	2	3	51	18	8	6	7	34	35	80
4	Manchester City	42	13	3	5	43	21	7	7	7	23	27	70
5	Grimsby Town	42	13	6	2	36	15	6	7	8	24	32	70
6	Blackburn Rovers	42	9	11	1	35	19	8	5	8	22	27	67
7	Carlisle United	42	10	9	2	29	13	6	7	8	19	28	64
8	Shrewsbury Town	42	13	5	3	34	18	4	5	12	15	35	61
9	Brighton & Hove Albion	42	11	6	4	42	17	6	3	12	27	43	60
10	Leeds United	42	13	4	4	33	16	3	8	10	22	40	60
11	Fulham	42	9	6	6	35	24	6	6	9	25	29	57
12	Huddersfield Town	42	8	6	7	27	20	6	6	6	29	29	57
13	Charlton Athletic	42	13	4	4	40	26	3	5	13	13	38	57
14	Barnsley	42	9	6	6	33	23	6	1	14	24	30	52
15	Cardiff City	42	11	3	7	32	27	4	3	14	21	39	51

16	Portsmouth	42	8	3	10	46	32	6	4	11	27	32	49
17	Middlesbrough	42	9	8	4	26	18	3	5	13	15	29	49
18	Crystal Palace	42	8	5	8	18	18	4	6	11	24	34	47
19	Oldham Athletic	42	10	6	5	33	27	3	2	16	14	46	47
20	Derby County	42	9	5	7	26	26	2	4	15	10	46	42
21	Swansea City	42	7	4	10	20	28	0	4	17	16	57	29
22	Cambridge United	42	4	7	10	20	33	0	5	16	8	44	24

Canon League Division 3

		P	W	D	L	F	A	W	D	L	F	A	Pts
1	Oxford United	46	17	5	1	58	22	11	6	6	33	28	95
2	Wimbledon	46	15	5	3	58	35	11	4	8	39	41	87
3	Sheffield United	46	14	7	2	56	18	10	4	9	30	35	83
4	Hull City	46	16	5	2	42	11	7	9	7	29	27	83
5	Bristol Rovers	46	16	5	2	47	21	6	8	9	21	33	79
6	Walsall	46	14	4	5	44	22	8	5	10	24	39	75
7	Bradford City	46	11	9	3	46	30	9	2	12	27	35	71
8	Gillingham	46	13	4	6	50	29	7	6	10	24	40	70
9	Millwall	46	16	4	3	42	18	2	9	12	29	47	67
10	Bolton Wanderers	46	13	4	6	36	17	5	6	12	20	43	64
11	Leyton Orient	46	13	5	5	40	27	5	4	14	31	54	63
12	Burnley	46	12	5	6	52	25	4	9	10	24	36	62

		P	W	D	L	F	A	W	D	L	F	A	Pts
13	Newport County	46	11	9	3	35	27	5	5	13	23	48	62
14	Lincoln City	46	11	4	8	42	29	6	6	11	17	33	61
15	Wigan Athletic	46	11	5	7	26	18	5	8	10	20	38	61
16	Preston North End	46	12	5	6	42	27	3	6	14	24	39	56
17	Bournemouth	46	11	5	7	38	27	5	2	16	25	46	55
18	Rotherham United	46	10	5	8	29	17	5	4	14	28	47	54
19	Plymouth Argyle	46	11	5	4	38	17	2	4	17	18	45	51
20	Brentford	46	8	9	6	41	30	3	7	13	28	49	49
21	Scunthorpe United	46	9	9	5	40	31	0	10	13	14	42	46
22	Southend United	46	8	9	6	34	24	2	5	16	21	52	44
23	Port Vale	46	10	4	9	33	29	1	6	16	18	54	43
24	Exeter City	46	4	8	11	27	39	2	7	14	23	45	33

Canon League Division 4

		P	W	D	L	F	A	W	D	L	F	A	Pts
1	York City	46	18	4	1	58	16	13	4	6	38	23	101
2	Doncaster Rovers	46	15	6	2	46	22	9	7	7	36	32	85
3	Reading	46	17	6	0	51	14	5	10	8	33	42	82
4	Bristol City	46	18	3	2	51	17	6	7	10	19	27	82
5	Aldershot	46	14	6	3	49	29	8	3	12	27	40	75
6	Blackpool	46	15	4	4	47	19	6	5	12	23	33	72
7	Peterborough United	46	15	5	3	52	16	3	9	11	20	32	68

Pos	Team	P	W	D	L	F	A	W	D	L	F	A	Pts
8	Colchester United	46	14	7	2	45	14	3	9	11	24	39	67
9	Torquay United	46	13	7	3	32	18	5	6	12	27	46	67
10	Tranmere Rovers	46	11	5	7	33	26	6	10	7	20	27	66
11	Hereford United	46	11	6	6	31	21	5	9	9	23	32	63
12	Stockport County	46	12	5	6	34	25	5	6	12	26	39	62
13	Chesterfield	46	10	11	2	34	24	5	4	14	25	37	60
14	Darlington	46	13	4	6	31	19	4	4	15	18	31	59
15	Bury	46	9	7	7	34	32	6	7	10	27	32	59
16	Crewe Alexandra	46	10	8	5	35	27	6	3	14	21	40	59
17	Swindon Town	46	11	7	5	34	23	4	6	13	24	33	58
18	Northampton	46	10	8	5	32	32	3	6	14	21	46	53
19	Mansfield Town	46	9	7	7	44	27	4	6	13	22	43	52
20	Wrexham	46	7	6	10	34	33	4	9	10	25	41	48
21	Halifax Town	46	11	6	6	36	25	1	6	16	19	64	48
22	Rochdale	46	8	9	6	35	31	3	4	16	17	49	46
23	Hartlepool United	46	7	8	8	31	28	3	2	18	16	57	40
24	Chester City	46	7	5	11	23	35	0	8	15	22	47	34

Season 1984/85

Canon League Division 1

		P	W	D	L	F	A	W	D	L	F	A	Pts
1	Everton	42	16	3	2	58	17	12	3	6	30	26	90
2	Liverpool	42	12	4	5	36	19	10	7	4	32	16	77
3	Tottenham Hotspur	42	11	3	7	46	31	12	5	4	32	20	77
4	Manchester United	42	13	6	2	47	13	9	4	8	30	34	76
5	Southampton	42	13	4	4	29	18	6	7	8	27	29	68
6	Chelsea	42	13	3	5	38	20	5	9	7	25	28	66
7	Arsenal	42	14	5	2	37	14	5	4	12	24	35	66
8	Sheffield Wednesday	42	12	7	2	39	21	5	7	9	19	24	65
9	Nottingham Forest	42	13	4	4	35	18	6	3	12	21	30	64
10	Aston Villa	42	10	7	4	34	20	5	4	12	26	40	56
11	Watford	42	10	5	6	48	30	4	8	9	33	41	55
12	West Bromwich Albion	42	11	4	6	36	23	5	3	13	22	39	55
13	Luton Town	42	12	5	4	40	22	3	4	14	17	39	54
14	Newcastle United	42	11	4	6	33	26	2	9	10	22	44	52
15	Leicester City	42	10	4	7	39	25	5	2	14	26	48	51
16	West Ham United	42	7	8	6	27	23	6	4	11	24	45	51
17	Ipswich Town	42	8	7	6	27	20	5	4	12	19	37	50
18	Coventry City	42	11	3	7	29	22	4	2	15	18	42	50

		P	W	D	L	F	A	W	D	L	F	A	Pts
19	Queens Park Rangers	42	11	6	4	41	30	2	5	14	12	42	50
20	Norwich City	42	9	6	6	28	24	4	4	13	18	40	49
21	Sunderland	42	7	6	8	20	26	3	4	14	20	36	40
22	Stoke City	42	3	3	15	18	41	0	5	16	6	50	17

Canon League Division 2

		P	W	D	L	F	A	W	D	L	F	A	Pts
1	Oxford United	42	18	2	1	62	15	7	7	7	22	21	84
2	Birmingham City	42	12	6	3	30	15	13	1	7	29	18	82
3	Manchester City	42	14	4	3	42	16	7	7	7	24	24	74
4	Portsmouth	42	11	6	4	39	25	9	8	4	30	25	74
5	Blackburn Rovers	42	14	3	4	38	15	7	7	7	28	26	73
6	Brighton & Hove Albion	42	13	6	2	31	11	7	6	8	23	23	72
7	Leeds United	42	12	7	2	37	11	7	5	9	29	32	69
8	Shrewsbury Town	42	12	6	3	45	22	6	5	10	21	31	65
9	Fulham	42	13	3	5	35	26	6	5	10	33	38	65
10	Grimsby Town	42	13	1	7	47	32	5	7	9	25	32	62
11	Barnsley	42	11	7	3	27	12	3	9	9	15	30	58
12	Wimbledon	42	9	8	4	40	29	7	2	12	31	46	58
13	Huddersfield Town	42	9	5	7	28	29	6	5	10	24	35	55
14	Oldham Athletic	42	10	4	7	27	23	5	4	12	22	44	53
15	Crystal Palace	42	8	7	6	25	27	4	5	12	21	38	48

		P	W	D	L	F	A	W	D	L	F	A	Pts
16	Carlisle United	42	8	5	8	27	23	5	3	13	23	44	47
17	Charlton Athletic	42	8	7	6	34	30	3	5	13	17	33	45
18	Sheffield United	42	7	6	8	31	28	3	8	10	23	38	44
19	Middlesbrough	42	6	8	7	22	26	4	2	15	19	31	40
20	Notts County	42	6	5	10	25	32	4	2	15	20	41	37
21	Cardiff City	42	5	3	13	24	42	4	5	12	23	37	35
22	Wolverhampton Wanderers	42	5	4	12	18	32	3	5	13	19	47	33

Canon League Division 3

		P	W	D	L	F	A	W	D	L	F	A	Pts
1	Bradford City	46	15	6	2	44	23	13	4	6	33	22	94
2	Millwall	46	18	5	0	44	12	8	7	8	29	30	90
3	Hull City	46	16	4	3	46	20	9	8	6	32	29	87
4	Gillingham	46	15	5	3	54	29	10	3	10	26	33	83
5	Bristol City	46	17	2	4	46	19	7	7	9	28	28	81
6	Bristol Rovers	46	15	6	2	37	13	6	6	11	29	35	75
7	Derby County	46	14	7	2	40	20	5	6	12	25	34	70
8	York City	46	13	5	5	42	22	7	4	12	28	35	69
9	Reading	46	8	7	8	31	29	11	5	7	37	33	69
10	Bournemouth	46	16	3	4	42	16	3	8	12	15	30	68
11	Walsall	46	9	7	7	33	22	9	6	8	25	30	67
12	Rotherham United	46	11	6	6	36	24	7	5	11	19	31	65

		P	W	D	L	F	A	W	D	L	F	A	Pts
13	Brentford	46	13	5	5	42	27	3	9	11	20	37	62
14	Doncaster Rovers	46	11	5	7	42	33	6	3	14	30	41	59
15	Plymouth Argyle	46	11	7	5	33	23	4	7	12	29	42	59
16	Wigan Athletic	46	12	6	5	36	22	3	8	12	24	42	59
17	Bolton Wanderers	46	12	5	6	38	22	4	1	18	31	53	54
18	Newport County	46	9	6	8	30	30	4	7	12	25	37	52
19	Lincoln City	46	8	11	4	32	20	3	7	13	18	31	51
20	Swansea City	46	7	5	11	31	39	3	7	12	22	41	47
21	Burnley	46	6	8	9	30	24	5	6	13	30	49	46
22	Leyton Orient	46	7	7	9	30	36	4	6	13	21	40	46
23	Preston North End	46	9	5	9	33	41	4	2	17	18	59	46
24	Cambridge United	46	2	3	18	17	48	2	6	15	20	47	21

*Bradford City v. Lincoln City was abandoned after forty minutes; the result stands.

Canon League Division 4

		P	W	D	L	F	A	W	D	L	F	A	Pts
1	Chesterfield	46	16	6	1	40	13	10	7	6	24	22	91
2	Blackpool	46	15	7	1	42	15	9	7	7	31	24	86
3	Darlington	46	16	4	3	41	22	8	9	6	25	27	85
4	Bury	46	15	6	2	46	20	9	6	8	30	30	84

Pos	Team	P	W	D	L	F	A	W	D	L	F	A	Pts
5	Hereford United	46	16	2	5	38	21	6	9	8	27	26	77
6	Tranmere Rovers	46	17	1	5	50	21	7	2	14	33	45	75
7	Colchester United	46	13	7	3	49	29	7	7	9	38	36	74
8	Swindon Town	46	16	4	3	42	21	5	5	13	20	37	72
9	Scunthorpe United	46	14	6	3	61	33	5	8	10	22	29	71
10	Crewe Alexandra	46	10	7	6	32	28	8	5	10	33	41	66
11	Peterborough United	46	11	7	5	29	21	5	7	11	25	32	62
12	Port Vale	46	11	8	4	39	24	3	10	10	22	35	60
13	Aldershot	46	11	6	6	33	20	6	2	15	23	43	59
14	Mansfield Town	46	10	8	5	25	15	3	10	10	16	23	57
15	Wrexham	46	10	6	7	39	27	5	3	15	28	43	54
16	Chester City	46	11	3	9	35	30	4	6	13	25	42	54
17	Rochdale	46	8	7	8	33	30	5	7	11	22	39	53
18	Exeter City	46	9	7	7	30	27	4	7	12	27	52	53
19	Hartlepool United	46	10	6	7	34	29	4	4	15	20	38	52
20	Southend United	46	8	8	7	30	34	5	3	15	28	49	50
21	Halifax Town	46	9	3	11	26	32	6	2	15	16	37	50
22	Stockport County	46	11	5	7	40	26	2	3	18	18	53	47
23	Northampton	46	10	1	12	32	32	4	4	15	21	42	47
24	Torquay United	46	5	11	7	18	24	4	3	16	20	39	41

Season 1985/86

Canon League Division 1

		P	W	D	L	F	A	W	D	L	F	A	Pts
1	Liverpool	42	16	4	1	58	14	10	6	5	31	23	88
2	Everton	42	16	3	2	54	18	10	5	6	33	23	86
3	West Ham United	42	17	2	2	48	16	9	4	8	26	24	84
4	Manchester United	42	12	5	4	35	12	10	5	6	35	24	76
5	Sheffield Wednesday	42	13	6	2	36	23	8	4	9	27	31	73
6	Chelsea	42	12	4	5	32	27	8	7	6	25	29	71
7	Arsenal	42	13	5	3	29	15	7	4	10	20	32	69
8	Nottingham Forest	42	11	5	5	38	25	8	6	7	31	28	68
9	Luton Town	42	12	6	3	37	15	6	6	9	24	29	66
10	Tottenham Hotspur	42	12	2	7	47	25	7	6	8	27	27	65
11	Newcastle United	42	12	5	4	46	31	5	7	9	21	41	63
12	Watford	42	11	6	4	40	22	5	5	11	29	40	59
13	Queen's Park Rangers	42	12	3	6	33	20	3	4	14	20	44	52
14	Southampton	42	10	6	5	32	18	2	4	15	19	44	46
15	Manchester City	42	7	7	7	25	26	4	5	12	18	31	45
16	Aston Villa	42	7	6	8	27	28	3	8	10	24	39	44
17	Coventry City	42	6	5	10	31	35	5	5	11	17	36	43

		P	W	D	L	F	A	W	D	L	F	A	Pts
18	Oxford United	42	7	7	7	34	27	3	5	13	28	53	42
19	Leicester City	42	7	8	6	35	35	3	4	14	19	41	42
20	Ipswich Town	42	8	5	8	20	24	3	3	15	12	31	41
21	Birmingham City	42	5	2	14	13	25	3	3	15	17	48	29
22	West Bromwich Albion	42	3	8	10	21	36	1	4	16	14	53	24

Canon League Division 2

		P	W	D	L	F	A	W	D	L	F	A	Pts
1	Norwich City	42	16	4	1	51	15	9	5	7	33	22	84
2	Charlton Athletic	42	14	5	2	44	15	8	6	7	34	30	77
3	Wimbledon	42	13	6	2	38	16	8	7	6	20	21	76
4	Portsmouth	42	13	4	4	43	17	9	3	9	26	24	73
5	Crystal Palace	42	12	3	6	29	22	7	6	8	28	30	66
6	Hull City	42	11	7	3	39	19	6	6	9	26	36	64
7	Sheffield United	42	10	7	4	36	24	7	4	10	28	39	62
8	Oldham Athletic	42	13	4	4	40	28	4	5	12	22	33	60
9	Millwall	42	12	3	6	39	24	5	5	11	25	41	59
10	Stoke City	42	8	11	2	29	16	6	4	11	19	34	57
11	Brighton & Hove Albion	42	10	5	6	42	30	6	3	12	22	34	56
12	Barnsley	42	9	6	6	29	26	5	8	8	18	24	56
13	Bradford City	42	14	1	6	36	24	2	5	14	15	39	54
14	Leeds United	42	9	7	5	30	22	6	1	14	26	50	53

		P	W	D	L	F	A	W	D	L	F	A	Pts
15	Grimsby Town	42	11	4	6	35	24	3	6	12	23	38	52
16	Huddersfield Town	42	10	6	5	30	23	4	4	13	21	44	52
17	Shrewsbury Town	42	11	5	5	29	20	3	4	14	23	44	51
18	Sunderland	42	10	5	6	33	29	3	6	12	14	32	50
19	Blackburn Rovers	42	10	4	7	30	20	2	9	10	23	42	49
20	Carlisle United	42	10	2	9	30	28	3	5	13	17	43	46
21	Middlesbrough	42	8	6	7	26	23	4	3	14	18	30	45
22	Fulham	42	8	3	10	29	32	2	3	16	16	37	36

Canon League Division 3

		P	W	D	L	F	A	W	D	L	F	A	Pts
1	Reading	46	16	3	4	39	22	13	4	6	28	29	94
2	Plymouth Argyle	46	17	3	3	56	20	9	6	8	32	33	87
3	Derby County	46	13	7	3	45	20	10	8	5	35	21	84
4	Wigan Athletic	46	17	4	2	54	17	6	10	7	28	31	83
5	Gillingham	46	14	5	4	48	17	8	8	7	33	37	79
6	Walsall	46	15	7	1	59	23	7	2	14	31	41	75
7	York City	46	16	4	3	49	17	4	7	12	28	41	71
8	Notts County	46	12	6	5	42	26	7	8	8	29	34	71
9	Bristol City	46	14	5	4	43	19	4	9	10	26	41	68
10	Brentford	46	8	8	7	29	29	10	4	9	29	32	66

		P	W	D	L	F	A	W	D	L	F	A	Pts
11	Doncaster Rovers	46	7	10	6	20	21	9	6	8	25	31	64
12	Blackpool	46	11	6	6	38	19	6	6	11	28	36	63
13	Darlington	46	10	7	6	39	33	5	6	12	22	45	58
14	Rotherham United	46	13	5	5	44	18	2	7	14	17	41	57
15	Bournemouth	46	9	6	8	41	31	6	3	14	24	41	54
16	Bristol Rovers	46	9	8	6	27	21	5	4	14	24	54	54
17	Chesterfield	46	10	6	7	41	30	3	8	12	20	34	53
18	Bolton Wanderers	46	10	4	9	35	30	5	4	14	19	38	53
19	Newport County	46	7	8	8	35	33	4	10	9	17	32	51
20	Bury	46	11	7	5	46	26	1	6	16	17	41	49
21	Lincoln City	46	7	9	7	33	34	3	7	13	22	43	46
22	Cardiff City	46	7	5	11	22	29	5	4	14	31	54	45
23	Wolverhampton Wanderers	46	6	6	11	29	47	5	4	14	28	51	43
24	Swansea City	46	9	6	8	27	27	2	4	17	16	60	43

Canon League Division 4

		P	W	D	L	F	A	W	D	L	F	A	Pts
1	Swindon Town	46	20	2	1	52	19	12	4	7	30	24	102
2	Chester City	46	15	5	3	44	16	8	10	5	39	34	84
3	Mansfield Town	46	13	8	2	43	17	10	4	9	31	30	81
4	Port Vale	46	13	9	1	42	11	8	7	8	25	26	79
5	Leyton Orient	46	11	6	6	39	21	9	6	8	40	43	72

6	Colchester United	46	12	6	5	51	22	7	7	9	37	41	70
7	Hartlepool United	46	15	6	2	41	20	5	4	14	27	47	70
8	Northampton	46	9	7	7	44	29	9	3	11	35	29	64
9	Southend United	46	13	4	6	43	27	5	6	12	26	40	64
10	Hereford United	46	15	6	2	55	30	3	4	16	19	43	64
11	Stockport County	46	9	9	5	35	28	8	4	11	28	43	64
12	Crewe Alexandra	46	10	6	7	35	26	8	3	12	19	35	63
13	Wrexham	46	11	5	7	34	24	6	4	13	34	56	60
14	Burnley	46	11	3	9	35	30	5	8	10	25	35	59
15	Scunthorpe United	46	11	7	5	33	23	4	7	12	17	32	59
16	Aldershot	46	12	5	6	45	25	5	2	16	21	49	58
17	Peterborough United	46	9	11	3	31	19	4	6	13	21	45	56
18	Rochdale	46	12	7	4	41	29	2	6	15	16	48	55
19	Tranmere Rovers	46	9	1	13	46	41	6	8	9	28	32	54
20	Halifax Town	46	10	8	5	35	27	4	4	15	25	44	54
21	Exeter City	46	10	4	9	26	25	3	11	9	21	34	54
22	Cambridge United	46	12	2	9	45	38	3	7	13	20	42	54
23	Preston North End	46	7	4	12	32	41	4	6	13	22	48	43
24	Torquay United	46	8	5	10	29	32	1	5	17	14	56	37

Season 1986/87

Today League Division 1

		P	W	D	L	F	A	W	D	L	F	A	Pts
1	Everton	42	16	4	1	49	11	10	4	7	27	20	86
2	Liverpool	42	15	3	3	43	16	8	5	8	29	26	77
3	Tottenham Hotspur	42	14	3	4	40	14	7	5	9	28	29	71
4	Arsenal	42	12	5	4	31	12	8	5	8	27	23	70
5	Norwich City	42	9	10	2	27	20	8	7	6	26	31	68
6	Wimbledon	42	11	5	5	32	22	8	4	9	25	28	66
7	Luton Town	42	14	5	2	29	13	4	7	10	18	32	66
8	Nottingham Forest	42	12	8	1	36	14	6	3	12	28	37	65
9	Watford	42	12	5	4	38	20	6	4	11	29	34	63
10	Coventry City	42	14	4	3	35	17	3	8	10	15	28	63
11	Manchester United	42	13	3	5	38	18	1	11	9	14	27	56
12	Southampton	42	11	5	5	44	24	3	5	13	25	44	52
13	Sheffield Wednesday	42	9	7	5	39	24	4	6	11	19	35	52
14	Chelsea	42	8	6	7	30	30	5	7	9	23	34	52
15	West Ham United	42	10	4	7	33	28	4	6	11	19	39	52
16	Queen's Park Rangers	42	9	7	5	31	27	4	4	13	17	37	50
17	Newcastle United	42	10	4	7	33	29	2	7	12	14	36	47
18	Oxford United	42	8	8	5	30	25	3	5	13	14	44	46

19	Charlton Athletic	42	7	7	7	26	22	4	4	13	19	33	44
20	Leicester City	42	9	7	5	39	24	2	2	17	15	52	42
21	Manchester City	42	8	6	7	28	24	0	9	12	8	33	39
22	Aston Villa	42	7	7	7	25	25	1	5	15	20	54	36

Today League Division 2

		P	W	D	L	F	A	W	D	L	F	A	Pts
1	Derby County	42	14	6	1	42	18	11	3	7	22	20	84
2	Portsmouth	42	17	2	2	37	11	6	7	8	16	17	78
3	Oldham Athletic	42	13	6	2	36	16	9	3	9	29	28	75
4	Leeds United	42	15	4	2	43	16	4	7	10	15	28	68
5	Ipswich Town	42	12	6	3	29	10	5	7	9	30	33	64
6	Crystal Palace	42	12	4	5	35	20	7	1	13	16	33	62
7	Plymouth Argyle	42	12	6	3	40	23	4	7	10	22	34	61
8	Stoke City	42	11	5	5	40	21	5	5	11	23	32	58
9	Sheffield United	42	10	8	3	31	19	5	5	11	19	30	58
10	Bradford City	42	10	5	6	36	27	5	5	11	26	35	55
11	Barnsley	42	8	7	6	26	23	6	6	9	23	29	55
12	Blackburn Rovers	42	11	4	6	30	22	4	6	11	15	33	55
13	Reading	42	11	4	6	33	23	3	7	11	19	36	53
14	Hull City	42	10	6	5	25	22	3	8	10	16	33	53
15	West Bromwich Albion	42	8	6	7	29	22	5	6	10	22	27	51

16	Millwall	42	10	5	6	27	16	4	4	13	12	29	51
17	Huddersfield Town	42	9	6	6	38	30	6	4	11	16	31	51
18	Shrewsbury Town	42	11	3	7	24	14	3	4	14	17	39	51
19	Birmingham City	42	8	9	4	27	21	8	3	10	20	38	50
20	Sunderland	42	8	6	7	25	23	6	4	11	24	36	48
21	Grimsby Town	42	5	8	8	18	21	6	5	10	21	38	44
22	Brighton & Hove Albion	42	7	6	8	22	20	6	2	13	15	34	39

Today League Division 3

		P	W	D	L	F	A	W	D	L	F	A	Pts
1	Bournemouth	46	19	3	1	44	14	10	7	6	32	26	97
2	Middlesbrough	46	16	5	2	38	11	12	5	6	29	19	94
3	Swindon Town	46	14	5	4	37	19	11	7	5	40	28	87
4	Wigan Athletic	46	15	5	3	47	26	10	5	8	36	34	85
5	Gillingham	46	16	5	2	42	14	7	4	12	23	34	78
6	Bristol City	46	14	6	3	42	15	7	8	8	21	21	77
7	Notts County	46	14	6	3	52	24	7	7	9	25	32	76
8	Walsall	46	16	4	3	50	27	6	5	12	30	40	75
9	Blackpool	46	11	7	5	35	20	5	9	9	39	39	64
10	Mansfield Town	46	9	9	5	30	23	6	7	10	22	32	61
11	Brentford	46	9	7	7	39	32	6	8	9	25	34	60

		P	W	D	L	F	A	W	D	L	F	A	Pts
12	Port Vale	46	8	6	9	43	36	7	6	10	33	34	57
13	Doncaster Rovers	46	11	8	4	32	19	3	7	13	24	43	57
14	Rotherham United	46	10	6	7	29	23	5	6	12	19	34	57
15	Chester City	46	7	9	7	32	28	6	8	9	29	31	56
16	Bury	46	9	7	7	30	26	5	6	12	24	34	55
17	Chesterfield	46	11	5	7	36	33	2	10	11	20	36	54
18	Fulham	46	8	8	7	35	41	4	9	10	24	36	53
19	Bristol Rovers	46	7	8	8	26	29	6	4	13	23	46	51
20	York City	46	11	8	4	34	29	1	5	17	21	50	49
21	Bolton Wanderers	46	8	5	10	29	26	2	10	11	17	32	45
22	Carlisle United	46	7	5	11	26	35	3	3	17	13	43	38
23	Darlington	46	6	10	7	25	28	1	6	16	20	49	37
24	Newport County	46	4	9	10	26	34	4	4	15	23	52	37

Today League Division 4

		P	W	D	L	F	A	W	D	L	F	A	Pts
1	*Northampton*	46	20	2	1	56	20	10	7	6	47	33	99
2	*Preston North End*	46	16	4	3	36	18	10	8	5	36	29	90
3	*Southend United*	46	14	4	5	43	27	11	1	11	25	28	80
4	*Wolverhampton Wanderers*	46	12	3	8	36	24	12	4	7	33	26	79
5	*Colchester United*	46	15	3	5	41	20	6	4	13	23	36	70

		P	W	D	L	F	A	W	D	L	F	A	Pts
6	Aldershot	46	13	5	5	40	22	7	5	11	24	35	70
7	Leyton Orient	46	15	2	6	40	25	5	7	11	24	36	69
8	Scunthorpe United	46	15	3	5	52	27	3	9	11	21	30	66
9	Wrexham	46	8	13	2	38	24	7	7	9	32	27	65
10	Peterborough United	46	10	7	6	29	21	7	7	9	28	29	65
11	Cambridge United	46	12	6	5	37	23	5	5	13	23	39	62
12	Swansea City	46	13	3	7	31	21	4	8	11	25	40	62
13	Cardiff City	46	6	12	5	24	18	9	4	10	24	32	61
14	Exeter City	46	11	10	2	37	17	0	13	10	16	32	56
15	Halifax Town	46	10	5	8	32	32	5	5	13	27	42	55
16	Hereford United	46	10	6	7	33	23	4	5	14	27	38	53
17	Crewe Alexandra	46	8	9	6	38	35	5	5	13	32	37	53
18	Hartlepool United	46	6	11	6	24	30	5	7	11	20	35	51
19	Stockport County	46	9	6	8	25	27	4	6	13	15	42	51
20	Tranmere Rovers	46	6	10	7	32	37	5	7	11	22	35	50
21	Rochdale	46	8	8	7	31	30	3	9	11	23	43	50
22	Burnley	46	9	7	7	31	35	3	6	14	22	39	49
23	Torquay United	46	8	8	7	28	29	2	10	11	28	43	48
24	Lincoln City	46	8	7	8	30	27	4	5	14	15	38	48

Season 1987/88

Barclays League Division 1

		P	W	D	L	F	A	W	D	L	F	A	Pts
1	Liverpool	40	15	5	0	49	9	11	7	2	38	15	90
2	Manchester United	40	14	5	1	41	17	9	7	4	30	21	81
3	Nottingham Forest	40	11	7	2	40	17	9	6	5	27	22	73
4	Everton	40	14	4	2	34	11	5	9	6	19	16	70
5	Queen's Park Rangers	40	12	4	4	30	14	7	6	7	18	24	67
6	Arsenal	40	11	4	5	35	16	7	8	5	23	23	66
7	Wimbledon	40	8	9	3	32	20	6	6	8	26	27	57
8	Newcastle United	40	9	6	5	32	23	5	8	7	23	30	56
9	Luton Town	40	11	6	3	40	21	3	5	12	17	37	53
10	Coventry City	40	6	8	6	23	25	7	6	7	23	28	53
11	Sheffield Wednesday	40	10	2	8	27	30	5	6	9	25	36	53
12	Southampton	40	6	8	6	27	26	6	6	8	22	27	50
13	Tottenham Hotspur	40	9	5	6	26	23	3	6	11	12	25	47
14	Norwich City	40	7	5	8	26	26	5	4	11	14	26	45
15	Derby County	40	6	7	7	18	17	4	6	10	17	28	43
16	West Ham United	40	6	9	5	23	21	3	6	11	17	31	42
17	Charlton Athletic	40	7	7	6	23	21	2	8	10	15	31	42

18	Chelsea	40	7	11	2	24	17	2	4	14	26	51	42
19	Portsmouth	40	4	8	8	21	27	3	6	11	15	39	35
20	Watford	40	4	5	11	15	24	3	6	11	12	27	32
21	Oxford United	40	5	7	8	24	34	1	6	13	20	46	31

Barclays League Division 2

		P	W	D	L	F	A	W	D	L	F	A	Pts
1	Millwall	44	15	3	4	45	23	10	4	8	27	29	82
2	Aston Villa	44	9	7	6	31	21	13	5	4	37	20	78
3	Middlesbrough	44	15	4	3	44	16	7	8	7	19	20	78
4	Bradford City	44	14	3	5	49	26	8	8	6	25	28	77
5	Blackburn Rovers	44	12	8	2	38	22	9	6	7	30	30	77
6	Crystal Palace	44	16	3	3	50	21	6	6	10	36	38	75
7	Leeds United	44	14	4	4	37	18	5	8	9	24	33	69
8	Ipswich Town	44	14	3	5	38	17	5	6	11	23	35	66
9	Manchester City	44	11	4	7	50	28	8	4	10	30	32	65
10	Oldham Athletic	44	13	4	5	43	27	5	7	10	29	37	65
11	Stoke City	44	12	6	4	34	22	5	5	12	16	35	62
12	Swindon Town	44	10	7	5	43	25	6	4	12	30	35	59
13	Leicester City	44	12	5	5	35	20	4	6	12	27	41	59
14	Barnsley	44	11	4	7	42	32	4	8	10	19	30	57

		P	W	D	L	F	A	W	D	L	F	A	Pts
15	Hull City	44	10	8	4	32	22	4	7	11	22	38	57
16	Plymouth Argyle	44	12	4	6	44	26	4	4	14	21	41	56
17	Bournemouth	44	7	7	8	36	30	6	3	13	20	38	49
18	Shrewsbury Town	44	7	8	7	23	22	4	8	10	19	32	49
19	Birmingham City	44	7	9	6	20	24	4	6	12	21	42	48
20	West Bromwich Albion	44	8	7	7	29	26	4	4	14	21	43	47
21	Sheffield United	44	8	6	8	27	28	5	1	16	18	46	46
22	Reading	44	5	7	10	20	25	5	5	12	24	45	42
23	Huddersfield Town	44	4	6	12	20	38	2	4	16	21	62	28

Barclays League Division 3

		P	W	D	L	F	A	W	D	L	F	A	Pts
1	Sunderland	46	14	7	2	51	22	13	5	5	41	26	93
2	Brighton & Hove Albion	46	15	7	1	37	16	8	8	7	32	31	84
3	Walsall	46	15	6	2	39	22	8	7	8	29	28	82
4	Notts County	46	14	4	5	53	24	9	8	6	29	25	81
5	Bristol City	46	14	6	3	51	30	7	6	10	26	32	75
6	Northampton	46	12	8	3	36	18	6	11	6	34	33	73
7	Wigan Athletic	46	11	8	4	36	23	9	4	10	34	38	72
8	Bristol Rovers	46	14	5	4	43	19	4	7	12	25	37	66
9	Fulham	46	10	5	8	36	24	9	4	10	33	36	66

		P	W	D	L	F	A	W	D	L	F	A	Pts
10	Blackpool	46	13	4	6	45	27	4	10	9	26	35	65
11	Port Vale	46	12	8	3	36	19	6	3	14	22	37	65
12	Brentford	46	9	8	6	27	23	7	6	10	26	36	62
13	Gillingham	46	8	9	6	45	21	6	8	9	32	40	59
14	Bury	46	9	7	7	33	26	6	7	10	25	31	59
15	Chester City	46	9	8	6	29	30	5	8	10	22	32	58
16	Preston North End	46	10	6	7	30	23	5	7	11	18	36	58
17	Southend United	46	10	6	7	42	33	4	7	12	23	50	55
18	Chesterfield	46	10	5	8	25	28	5	5	13	16	42	55
19	Mansfield Town	46	10	6	7	25	21	4	6	13	23	38	54
20	Aldershot	46	12	3	8	45	32	3	5	15	19	42	53
21	Rotherham United	46	8	8	7	28	25	4	8	11	22	41	52
22	Grimsby Town	46	6	7	10	25	29	6	7	10	23	29	50
23	York City	46	4	7	12	27	45	4	2	17	21	46	33
24	Doncaster Rovers	46	6	5	12	25	36	2	4	17	15	48	33

Barclays League Division 4

		P	W	D	L	F	A	W	D	L	F	A	Pts
1	Wolverhampton Wanderers	46	15	3	5	47	19	12	6	5	35	24	90
2	Cardiff City	46	15	6	2	39	14	9	7	7	27	27	85
3	Bolton Wanderers	46	15	6	2	42	12	7	6	10	24	30	78
4	Scunthorpe United	46	14	5	4	42	20	6	12	5	34	31	77

5	Torquay United	46	10	7	6	34	16	11	7	5	32	25	77
6	Swansea City	46	9	7	7	35	28	11	3	9	27	28	70
7	Peterborough United	46	10	5	8	28	26	10	5	8	24	27	70
8	Leyton Orient	46	13	4	6	55	27	6	8	9	30	36	69
9	Colchester United	46	10	5	8	23	22	9	5	9	24	29	67
10	Burnley	46	12	5	6	31	22	8	2	13	26	40	67
11	Wrexham	46	13	3	7	46	26	7	3	13	23	32	66
12	Scarborough	46	12	8	3	38	19	5	6	12	18	29	65
13	Darlington	46	13	6	4	39	25	5	5	13	32	44	65
14	Tranmere Rovers	46	14	2	7	43	20	5	5	13	18	33	64
15	Cambridge United	46	10	6	7	32	24	6	7	10	18	28	61
16	Hartlepool United	46	9	7	7	25	19	6	7	10	25	32	59
17	Crewe Alexandra	46	7	11	5	25	19	6	8	9	32	34	58
18	Halifax Town	46	11	7	5	37	25	3	6	14	17	34	55
19	Hereford United	46	8	7	8	25	27	6	5	12	16	32	54
20	Stockport County	46	7	7	9	26	26	5	8	10	18	32	51
21	Rochdale	46	5	9	9	28	34	6	6	11	19	42	48
22	Exeter City	46	8	6	9	33	29	3	7	13	20	39	46
23	Carlisle United	46	9	5	9	38	33	3	3	17	19	53	44
24	*Newport County*	46	4	5	14	19	36	2	2	19	16	69	25

Season 1988/89

Barclays League Division 1

		P	W	D	L	F	A	W	D	L	F	A	Pts
1	Arsenal	38	10	6	3	35	19	12	4	3	38	17	76
2	Liverpool	38	11	5	3	33	11	11	5	3	32	17	76
3	Nottingham Forest	38	8	7	4	31	16	9	6	4	33	27	64
4	Norwich City	38	8	7	4	23	20	9	4	6	25	25	62
5	Derby County	38	9	3	7	23	18	8	4	7	17	20	58
6	Tottenham Hotspur	38	8	6	5	31	24	7	6	6	29	22	57
7	Coventry City	38	9	4	6	28	23	5	9	5	19	19	55
8	Everton	38	10	7	2	33	18	4	5	10	17	27	54
9	Queen's Park Rangers	38	9	5	5	23	16	5	6	8	20	21	53
10	Millwall	38	10	3	6	27	21	4	8	7	20	31	53
11	Manchester United	38	10	5	4	27	13	3	7	9	18	22	51
12	Wimbledon	38	10	3	6	30	19	4	6	9	20	27	51
13	Southampton	38	6	7	6	25	26	4	8	7	27	40	45
14	Charlton Athletic	38	6	7	6	25	24	4	5	10	19	34	42
15	Sheffield Wednesday	38	6	6	7	21	25	4	6	9	13	26	42
16	Luton Town	38	8	6	5	32	21	2	5	12	10	31	41
17	Aston Villa	38	7	6	6	25	22	2	7	10	20	34	40
18	*Middlesbrough*	38	6	7	6	28	30	3	5	11	16	31	39

		P	W	D	L	F	A	W	D	L	F	A	Pts
19	West Ham United	38	3	6	10	19	30	7	2	10	18	32	38
20	Newcastle United	38	3	6	11	19	28	4	4	11	13	35	31

Barclays League Division 2

		P	W	D	L	F	A	W	D	L	F	A	Pts
1	Chelsea	46	15	6	2	50	25	14	6	3	46	25	99
2	Manchester City	46	12	8	3	48	28	11	5	7	29	25	82
3	Crystal Palace	46	15	6	2	42	17	8	6	9	29	32	81
4	Watford	46	14	5	4	41	18	8	7	8	33	30	78
5	Blackburn Rovers	46	16	4	3	50	22	6	7	10	24	37	77
6	Swindon Town	46	13	8	2	35	15	7	8	8	33	38	76
7	Barnsley	46	12	8	3	37	21	8	6	9	29	37	74
8	Ipswich Town	46	13	3	7	42	23	9	4	10	29	38	73
9	West Bromwich Albion	46	13	7	3	43	18	5	11	7	22	23	72
10	Leeds United	46	12	6	5	34	20	5	10	8	25	30	67
11	Sunderland	46	12	8	3	40	23	4	7	12	20	37	63
12	Bournemouth	46	13	3	7	32	20	5	5	13	21	42	62
13	Stoke City	46	10	9	4	33	25	5	5	13	24	47	59
14	Bradford City	46	8	11	4	29	22	5	6	12	23	37	56
15	Leicester City	46	11	6	6	31	20	2	10	11	25	43	5
16	Oldham Athletic	46	9	10	4	49	32	2	11	10	26	40	54
17	Oxford United	46	11	6	6	40	34	3	6	14	22	36	54

18	Plymouth Argyle	46	11	4	8	35	22	3	8	12	20	44	54
19	Brighton & Hove Albion	46	11	5	7	36	24	3	4	16	21	42	51
20	Portsmouth	46	10	6	7	33	21	3	6	14	20	41	51
21	Hull City	46	7	9	7	31	25	4	5	14	21	43	47
22	Shrewsbury Town	46	4	11	8	25	31	4	7	12	15	36	42
23	Birmingham City	46	6	4	13	21	33	2	7	14	10	43	35
24	Walsall	46	3	10	10	27	42	2	6	15	14	38	31

Barclays League Division 3

		P	W	D	L	F	A	W	D	L	F	A	Pts
1	Wolverhampton Wanderers	46	18	4	1	61	19	8	10	5	35	30	92
2	Sheffield United	46	16	3	4	57	21	9	6	8	36	33	84
3	Port Vale	46	15	3	5	46	21	9	9	5	32	27	84
4	Fulham	46	12	7	4	42	28	10	2	11	27	39	75
5	Bristol Rovers	46	9	11	3	34	21	10	6	7	33	30	74
6	Preston North End	46	14	7	2	56	31	5	8	10	23	29	72
7	Brentford	46	14	5	4	36	21	4	9	10	30	40	68
8	Chester City	46	12	6	5	38	18	7	5	11	26	43	68
9	Notts County	46	11	7	5	37	22	7	6	10	27	32	67
10	Bolton Wanderers	46	12	8	3	42	23	4	8	11	16	31	64
11	Bristol City	46	10	3	10	32	25	8	6	9	21	30	63
12	Swansea City	46	11	8	4	33	22	4	8	11	18	31	61

		P	W	D	L	F	A	W	D	L	F	A	Pts
13	Bury	46	11	7	5	27	22	5	6	12	28	45	61
14	Huddersfield Town	46	10	8	5	35	25	7	1	15	28	48	60
15	Mansfield Town	46	10	8	5	32	22	4	9	10	16	30	59
16	Cardiff City	46	10	9	4	30	16	4	6	13	14	40	57
17	Wigan Athletic	46	9	5	9	28	22	5	9	9	27	31	56
18	Reading	46	10	6	7	37	29	5	5	13	31	43	56
19	Blackpool	46	10	6	7	36	29	4	7	12	20	30	55
20	Northampton	46	11	2	10	41	34	5	4	14	25	42	54
21	Southend United	46	10	9	4	33	26	3	6	14	23	49	54
22	Chesterfield	46	9	5	9	35	35	5	2	16	16	51	49
23	Gillingham	46	7	3	13	25	32	5	1	17	22	49	40
24	Aldershot	46	7	6	10	29	29	1	7	15	19	49	37

Barclays League Division 4

		P	W	D	L	F	A	W	D	L	F	A	Pts
1	Rotherham United	46	13	6	4	44	18	9	10	4	32	17	82
2	Tranmere Rovers	46	15	6	2	34	13	6	11	6	28	30	80
3	Crewe Alexandra	46	13	7	3	42	24	8	8	7	25	24	78
4	Scunthorpe United	46	11	9	3	40	22	10	5	8	37	35	77
5	Scarborough	46	12	7	4	33	23	9	7	7	34	29	77
6	Leyton Orient	46	16	2	5	61	19	5	10	8	25	31	75

7	Wrexham	46	12	7	4	44	28	7	7	9	33	35	71
8	Cambridge United	46	13	7	3	45	25	5	7	11	26	37	68
9	Grimsby Town	46	11	9	3	33	18	6	6	11	32	41	66
10	Lincoln City	46	12	6	5	39	26	6	4	13	25	34	64
11	York City	46	10	8	5	43	27	7	5	11	19	36	64
12	Carlisle United	46	9	6	8	26	25	6	9	8	27	27	60
13	Exeter City	46	14	4	5	46	23	4	2	17	19	45	60
14	Torquay United	46	15	2	6	32	23	2	6	15	13	37	59
15	Hereford United	46	11	8	4	40	27	3	8	12	26	45	58
16	Burnley	46	12	6	5	35	20	2	7	14	17	41	55
17	Peterborough United	46	10	3	10	29	32	4	9	10	23	42	54
18	Rochdale	46	10	10	3	32	26	3	4	16	24	56	53
19	Hartlepool United	46	10	6	7	33	33	4	4	15	17	45	52
20	Stockport County	46	8	10	5	31	20	2	11	10	23	32	51
21	Halifax Town	46	10	7	6	42	27	3	4	16	27	48	50
22	Colchester United	46	8	7	8	35	30	4	7	12	25	48	50
23	Doncaster Rovers	46	9	6	8	32	32	4	4	15	17	46	49
24	Darlington	46	3	12	8	28	38	5	6	12	25	38	42

HOME INTERNATIONALS

1979-80

	Pld	W	D	L	GF	GA	GD	Pts
Northern Ireland	3	2	1	0	3	1	+2	5
England	3	1	1	1	4	5	−1	3
Wales	3	1	0	2	4	3	+1	2
Scotland	3	1	0	2	1	3	−2	2

Northern Ireland	1 − 0	Scotland	(Hamilton)
Wales	4 − 1	England	(Thomas, Walsh, James, Thompson; Mariner)
England	1 − 1	Northern Ireland	(Brotherston og; Cochrane)
Scotland	1 − 0	Wales	(Miller)
Wales	0 − 1	Northern Ireland	(Brotherston)
Scotland	0 − 2	England	(Brooking, Coppell)

1980-81

	Pld	W	D	L	GF	GA	GD	Pts
Scotland	3	2	0	1	3	2	+1	4
Wales	2	1	1	0	2	0	+2	3
England	2	0	1	1	0	1	−1	1
Northern Ireland	1	0	0	1	0	2	−2	0

Wales	2 − 0	Scotland	(Walsh, Walsh)
Scotland	2 − 0	Northern Ireland	(Stewart, Archibald)
England	0 − 0	Wales	
England	0 − 1	Scotland	(Robertson)

The 1981 Home International championship was not completed due to security concerns in Northern Ireland which was experiencing times of heightened tension in The Troubles.

1981-82

	Pld	W	D	L	GF	GA	GD	Pts
England	3	3	0	0	6	0	+6	6
Scotland	3	1	1	1	3	3	0	3
Wales	3	1	0	2	3	2	+1	2
Northern Ireland	3	0	1	2	1	8	−7	1

England	4 − 0	Northern Ireland	(Robson, Keegan, Wilkins, Hoddle)
Wales	0 − 1	England	(Francis)
Northern Ireland	1 − 1	Scotland	(McIlroy; Wark)
Scotland	1 − 0	Wales	(Hartford)
Wales	3 − 0	Northern Ireland	(Curtis, Rush, Nicholas)
Scotland	0 − 1	England	(Mariner)

1982-83

	Pld	W	D	L	GF	GA	GD	Pts
England	3	2	1	0	4	1	+3	5
Scotland	3	1	1	1	2	2	0	3
Northern Ireland	3	0	2	1	0	1	−1	2
Wales	3	1	0	2	2	4	−2	2

England	2 − 1	Wales	(Butcher, Neal; Rush)
Scotland	0 − 0	Northern Ireland	
Northern Ireland	0 − 0	England	
Wales	0 − 2	Scotland	(Gray, Brazil)
Northern Ireland	0 − 1	Wales	(Davies)
England	2 − 0	Scotland	(Robson, Cowans)

1983-84

	Pld	W	D	L	GF	GA	GD	Pts
Northern Ireland	3	1	1	1	3	2	+1	3
Wales	3	1	1	1	3	3	0	3
England	3	1	1	1	2	2	0	3
Scotland	3	1	1	1	3	4	−1	3

Northern Ireland	2 − 0	Scotland	(Whiteside McIlroy)
Scotland	2 − 1	Wales	(Cooper, Johnston; James)
England	1 − 0	Northern Ireland	(Woodcock)
Wales	1 − 0	England	(Hughes)
Wales	1 − 1	Northern Ireland	(Hughes; Armstrong)
Scotland	1 − 1	England	(McGhee; Woodcock)

The 1984 Home International championship was the final one ever contested.

HONOURS

1979-80

European Championship	West Germany 2 Belgium 1
European Cup	Nottingham Forest 1 SV Hamburg 0
Division One Champions	Liverpool
Division Two Champions	Leicester City
Division Three Champions	Grimsby Town
Division Four Champions	Huddersfield Town
FA Cup	West Ham United 1 Arsenal 0
League Cup	Wolverhampton Wanderers 1 Nottingham Forest 0
European Cup Winners Cup	Valencia 0 Arsenal 0 (Valencia won 5-4 on penalties)
UEFA Cup	Eintract Frankfurt 3 Borussia Monchengladbach 3 (Eintract Frankfurt won on away goals; 3-2, 0-1)

1980-81

European Cup	Liverpool 1 Real Madrid 0
Division One Champions	Aston Villa
Division Two Champions	West Ham United
Division Three Champions	Rotherham United
Division Four Champions	Southend United
FA Cup	Tottenham Hotspur 3 Manchester City 2 (after 1-1 draw)
League Cup	Liverpool 2 West Ham United 1
European Cup Winners Cup	Dinamo Tbilisi 2 Carl Zeiss Jena 1
UEFA Cup	Ipswich Town 5 AZ Alkmaar 4 (on aggregate; 3-0, 2-4)

1981-82

World Cup	Italy 3 West Germany 1
European Cup	Aston Villa 1 Bayern Munich 0
Division One Champions	Liverpool
Division Two Champions	Luton Town
Division Three Champions	Burnley
Division Four Champions	Sheffield United
FA Cup	Tottenham Hotspur 1 Queens Park Rangers 0 (after 1–1 draw)
League Cup	Liverpool 3 Tottenham Hotspur 1
European Cup Winners Cup	Barcelona 2 Standard Liege 1
UEFA Cup	IFK Gothenburg 4 SV Hamburg 0 (on aggregate; 1–0, 3–0)

1982-83

European Cup	Hamburg 1 Juventus 0
Division One Champions	Liverpool
Division Two Champions	Queens Park Rangers
Division Three Champions	Portsmouth
Division Four Champions	Wimbledon
FA Cup	Manchester United 4 Brighton & Hove Albion 0 (after 2–2 draw)
League Cup	Liverpool 2 Manchester United 1
European Cup Winners Cup	Aberdeen 2 Real Madrid 1
UEFA Cup	Anderlecht 2 Benfica 1 (on aggregate; 1–0, 1–1)

1983-84

European Championship	France 2 Spain 0
European Cup	Liverpool 1 AS Roma 1 (Liverpool won 4–2 on penalties)
Division One Champions	Liverpool
Division Two Champions	Chelsea
Division Three Champions	Oxford United
Division Four Champions	York City
FA Cup	Everton 2 Watford 0

League Cup	Liverpool 1 Everton 0 (after 0-0 draw)
European Cup Winners Cup	Juventus 2 FC Porto 1
UEFA Cup	Tottenham Hotspur 2 Anderlecht 2 (on aggregate; 1-1, 1-1) (Tottenham Hotspur won 4-3 on penalties)

1984-85

European Cup	Juventus 1 Liverpool 0
Division One Champions	Everton
Division Two Champions	Oxford United
Division Three Champions	Bradford City
Division Four Champions	Chesterfield
FA Cup	Manchester United 1 Everton 0
League Cup	Norwich City 1 Sunderland 0
European Cup Winners Cup	Everton 3 Rapid Vienna 1
UEFA Cup	Real Madrid 3-1 Videoton (on aggregate; 3-0, 0-1)

1985-86

World Cup	Argentina 3 West Germany 2
European Cup	Steaua Bucharest 0 Barcelona 0 (Bucharest won 2-0 on penalties)
Division One Champions	Liverpool
Division Two Champions	Norwich City
Division Three Champions	Reading
Division Four Champions	Swindon Town
FA Cup	Liverpool 3 Everton 1
League Cup	Oxford United 3 Queens Park Rangers 0
European Cup Winners Cup	Dynamo Kiev 3 Atletico Madrid 0
UEFA Cup	Real Madrid 5 Cologne 3 (on aggregate; 5-1, 0-2)

1986-87

European Cup	Porto 2 Bayern Munich 1
Division One Champions	Everton
Division Two Champions	Derby County
Division Three Champions	Bournemouth
Division Four Champions	Northampton Town
FA Cup	Coventry City 3 Tottenham Hotspur 2
League Cup	Arsenal 2 Liverpool 1
European Cup Winners Cup	Ajax 1 Lokomotiv Leipzig 0
UEFA Cup	IFK Gothenburg 2 Dundee United 1 (on aggregate; 1-0, 1-1)

1987-88

European Championship	Holland 2 USSR 0
European Cup	PSV Eindhoven 0 Benfica 0 (PSV Eindhoven won 6-5 on penalties)
Division One Champions	Liverpool
Division Two Champions	Millwall
Division Three Champions	Sunderland
Division Four Champions	Wolverhampton Wanderers
FA Cup	Wimbledon 1 Liverpool 0
League Cup	Luton Town 3 Arsenal 2
European Cup Winners Cup	Mechelen 1 Ajax 0
UEFA Cup	Bayern Leverkusen 3 Espanol 3 (on aggregate; 0-3, 3-0) (Bayern Leverkusen won 3-2 on penalties)

1988-89

European Cup	AC Milan 4 Steaua Bucharest 0
Division One Champions	Arsenal
Division Two Champions	Chelsea
Division Three Champions	Wolverhampton Wanderers
Division Four Champions	Rotherham United
FA Cup	Liverpool 3 Everton 2
League Cup	Nottingham Forest 3 Luton Town 1
European Cup Winners Cup	Barcelona 2 Sampdoria 0
UEFA Cup	Napoli 5 VFB Stuttgart 4 (on aggregate; 2-1, 3-3)

PLAYERS OF THE YEAR

Footballer of the Year

1979–80	Terry McDermott	Liverpool
1980–81	Frans Thijssen	Ipswich Town
1981–82	Steve Perryman	Tottenham Hotspur
1982–83	Kenny Dalglish	Liverpool
1983–84	Ian Rush	Liverpool
1984–85	Neville Southall	Everton
1985–86	Gary Lineker	Everton
1986–87	Clive Allen	Tottenham Hotspur
1987–88	John Barnes	Liverpool
1988–89	Steve Nicol	Liverpool

PFA Players' Player of the Year

1979–80	Terry McDermott	Liverpool
1980–81	John Wark	Ipswich Town
1981–82	Kevin Keegan	Southampton
1982–83	Kenny Dalglish	Liverpool
1983–84	Ian Rush	Liverpool
1984–85	Peter Reid	Everton
1985–86	Gary Lineker	Everton
1986–87	Clive Allen	Tottenham Hotspur
1987–88	John Barnes	Liverpool
1988–89	Mark Hughes	Manchester United

PFA Young Player of the Year

1979–80	Glenn Hoddle	Tottenham Hotspur
1980–81	Gary Shaw	Aston Villa
1981–82	Steve Moran	Southampton
1982–83	Ian Rush	Liverpool
1983–84	Paul Walsh	Luton Town
1984–85	Mark Hughes	Manchester United
1985–86	Tony Cottee	West Ham United
1986–87	Tony Adams	Arsenal
1987–88	Paul Gascoigne	Newcastle United
1988–89	Paul Merson	Arsenal
1989–90	Matthew Le Tissier	Southampton

European Footballer of the Year

1980	Karl-Heinz Rumenigge	Bayern Munich
1981	Karl-Heinz Rumenigge	Bayern Munich
1982	Paolo Rossi	Juventus
1983	Michel Platini	Juventus
1984	Michel Platini	Juventus
1985	Michel Platini	Juventus
1986	Igor Belanov	Dynamo Kiev
1987	Ruud Gullit	AC Milan
1988	Marco Van Basten	AC Milan
1989	Marco Van Basten	AC Milan